THE WAR

ITS

CAUSES AND CONSEQUENCES.

BY

C. C. S. FARRAR,

OF BOLIVAR COUNTY, MISS.

BLELOCK & CO.:

CAIRO, ILLS.; MEMPHIS, TENN.; PADUCAH, KY.

1864.

CONTENTS.

PART I.

CAUSES OF THE WAR.

PART II.

CONSEQUENCES OF THE WAR.

THE WAR:

ITS CAUSES AND CONSEQUENCES.

2

PART I.

CAUSES OF THE WAR.

I. The Revolutionary Character of the Age.

FOR a solution of the war which is now afflicting us, we must look deeper than is customary. The cause does not lie so near the surface as is generally supposed. No doubt the immediate provocation is correctly assigned; but the negro agitation is symptomatic merely, and has been the occasion, not the cause, of the war. The disease, which is idiopathic, lies deep at the vitals of society, and is irremediable, because born of the social decompositions of the Age. If such a paradox be allowed, I should say it must kill before it can be cured, and society, like the phœnix, spring afresh from its own ashes. In other words, the malady resides in the fundamental principles of the government, and the remedy can come only by the slow corrections of time; that is, by a process of elimination and renewal. The development of the social evolution, according to the law of growth, will leave the disease behind, by carrying society out of the age to which it belongs. Every period of life has its own complaints; our society is yet in its infancy; it has many elements undeveloped, many organs that are merely rudimental. These elements and organs must come forth; they must take their places at the basis of government; they must have themselves represented by appropriate institutions, and be enabled to exercise their peculiar functions in determining the progress of the nation. These developments are seldom accomplished without shocks, more or less violent, to the social system. True science alone can mitigate the evil and facilitate the necessary parturitions; for they are, in a manner, new births, which society perpetually undergoes, and the highest art of which the human mind is capable is needed to aid its painful travails. The present is just such a paroxysm. The charlatanry now presiding at the national *accouchement* can only aggravate the throes of labor; and if society survive its ministrations, it may be thankful to its own imperishable vigor and the blind energies of nature.

The grand civilization of the world, so far from being finished, is but little more than just begun. In the manner of its development, it is still subjugated to the passions of mankind, and scarcely listens to the voice of reason. It is, therefore, yet in the epoch of its spontaneous movement, which is necessarily more or less erratic, and wars the almost inevitable consequence. When it shall enter upon its next stage—its reflective development—its course will be more steady, and wars, perhaps, if they cease not altogether, will at least give precedence to reason and reflection.

The civilization of this country, more special in its character and less grand and complicated in its movement, obeys the same laws which govern the development of the general civilization of the world, of which it is an episode, or rather a component part. It, too, like the other, unfolds by a compound action, and has its spontaneous and reflective modes of development. The former method, which answers to the youth of humanity, or to that early period of life which is given over to passion and impulse, is nearly always accompanied by violent revolutions, which seldom pass off without leaving behind them social changes of a radical nature, and depositing at the foundations of society principles other than those they found there.

These social cataclysms, beneficial in the long run, are generally destructive of those conditions of society which brought them on, and of the persons who conduct them. Like Saturn, they devour their own offspring, but leave in society, which is never entirely destroyed by them, the seeds of future improvements, which more or less time is needed to germinate and carry forward to institutions, which are their legitimate fruit.

This idea, under existing circumstances, is not consolatory to the present generation; but it is preventive of false hopes and consequent disappointments. The very knowledge of the existence of such a social fact, if we make use of it, might go a little way toward mitigating the evils of the times, and perhaps might hasten their ultimate eradication, and bring on an earlier substitution, at the base of society, of principles which the revolution requires in the place of those already there. Otherwise, if we persist in obstinate ignorance of it, many long years might be wasted by the *blind forces of nature* in accomplishing what a little reflection would show to be the obvious purpose of the revolution.

The hitherto undiscovered laws of a kind of social philosophy, which had such a powerful agency in destroying the institutions of past eras, are only just beginning to be suspected in our day; and the bare comprehension of the fact that such laws exist, constitutes the glory of our age. The application of these laws, so far as we know anything about them, might not be inappropriate at the present time; and an investigation of the fundamental principles of our society would doubtless aid us in whatever use we might see proper to make of them. The present is certainly a desperate crisis in our political affairs. If there be such a thing as a social science, capable of explaining our situation, and of rectifying the errors of an ignorant charlatanry which has brought us to this pass, now is the time and the occasion, if ever, for it to exert itself in our behalf.

We have long been in the habit of idolizing our form of government; of believing that it alone, of all other social systems, was capable of affording liberty, security, and happiness to mankind; and that society could enjoy order and progress only under the ægis of its political principles. It was deemed to have been organized with a special view to internal peace and domestic tranquillity; while it was not defective in capacity for successful resistance to external aggression. The opinion prevailed that revolutions, so common and ruinous in other countries, were utterly excluded by the terms of this organization; because, in a government where all the power is in the hands of the people—where, in short, the government and people are one and the same thing —there is nothing to revolutionize, and nobody to do it; for it was difficult to conceive how the people could rebel against themselves.

It was said that *power*, habitually in the hands of a whole community, loses all the ordinary associated ideas of power, for the want of opposition—something to operate upon. For example: we perceive no exertion of power in the motion of the planetary system, but a very strong one in the movement of a whirlwind; it is because we see obstructions in the latter, but none in the former. Where the government is *not* in the hands of the people, there you find opposition, you perceive two contending interests, and get an idea of the exercise of power; and whether this power be in the hands of the government or of the people, or whether it change from side to side, it is always to be dreaded. *Fixed* in the hands of the whole people, it was then thought to be destroyed forever.*

Another happy consequence of this political system was said to be the *facility of changing the structure of government*, whenever and as often as the society shall think there is anything in it to amend. This did indeed seem to be a wondrous faculty possessed by the system, and has been exercised so often that no room is left to doubt its existence. As for the capacity of the people for self-government, no question was made of it—it was assumed as a matter of course—and the *right* to govern themselves flowed as a necessary consequence from their *capacity* for that office.

These, and many others of like kind, were plausible arguments in the case, and were so agreeable to the sense of the people, that few were disposed to contradict them. But, as little as the thought has hitherto been

---

* See Joel Barlow's Political Writings.

entertained, yet it is true that the social condition of this country is, more than all others in the world, exposed to perturbations from its own organic principles; and the present war is but one of a series of shocks destined to convulse society here for a long time to come, unless its *radices*, its very roots are speedily extirpated, or their tendency to wasteful extravagance is effectually subdued.

The AGE is revolutionary. The present is an epoch in the world's history of transition — a sort of moral exodus of the nations—which has lasted now some three centuries; and no stability in governments anywhere, much less here, can be looked for until the passage from the old *regime* to the new has been completed.

To a close observer, the social ebullition in this country has long been of a threatening character. From the birth of our government, its elements have been in an uneasy state; and the bosom of society has more than once been agitated by the throes of coming convulsions. The time has arrived for these inevitable disturbances, so long concealed, to manifest their dangerous activity. An open rupture is at last reached; and however it may be allayed temporarily, will be again and again renewed until the foundations of society are broken up, or the principles which now lie at its base are extruded, or so modified by the introduction of others that their excesses will be entirely counteracted.

The novelty of this declaration will no doubt astonish many, and the announcement be received with general incredulity. But let no one jump to conclusions, or condemn without hearing. To convince this people of the insufficiency of the democratic principles to serve further the purposes of social order, will seem like convincing them of their own incapacity for self-government. Such a task would appear, at first view, to be a very difficult one; it will be thought an object from which the eloquence of the closet must shrink in despair, and which prudence would leave to the more powerful arguments of events. Those arguments are now being employed with disastrous effect; and however infallible may be the logic of the sword, the people would best evince their own capacity by removing at once the discussion to a more peaceful tribunal; as long as it remains where it is, the weight of evidence is largely against them. The force of circumstances, however efficacious in the long run, is a terrible remedy for social ills. It was not only to prevent the recurrence of those ills, but to obviate as well the necessity of employing so drastic an agency to remove them, that the democratic principles were substituted at the base of government. So far from fulfilling these designs, I expect to prove their complicity in the present treason against the peace of society, and to show that they have failed of accomplishing all the great ends expected of them. "When, in the natural course of events, any doctrine has become hostile to the purposes it was destined to serve, it is evidently done with; and its end, or the close of its activity, is near."

Institutions, as has so often been said, are nothing but opinions carried into practice. All governments rest upon sentiments that have become prevalent in a given epoch; and as ideas are, by their very nature, fluctuating and evanescent, no given form of civilization can endure forever: hence the mobility of society, the transformation of systems, and the destruction of nations. No doubt the notions that prevail for the time being, and help to determine the course of civilization, have always more or less of truth in them while they are current; for when an idea has subjugated any considerable number of minds, and has lasted so long and so well as to carry itself into the social structures of the age, it is clear it does so by virtue of the truth, not the error, that is in it. Its error generally consists in its exclusiveness; that is, in what it excludes, more than in what it contains. No single idea includes *all* truth; but there never was an idea yet that did not think itself the *whole* truth. It is false, therefore, in so far as it assumes to be absolute and universal, instead of relative and limited. Hence the evils that flow from it; and these evils are unavoidable in the present state of civilization; because all speculative ideas, which are the constituents of society, are intolerant and proscriptive. No idea will endure the presence of another which seems to limit its action; and political principles, like religious dogmas, are of all others the least patient of fellowship or restraint. When in power, it is not in the nature of things that they can practice forbearance and moderation; and their outbreaks are not unfrequently marked by the ruin of generations, and sometimes of nations. If, therefore, we would know the origin of the social ills that afflict a given epoch or nation, we must penetrate to the bottom of its society, and seek for them in the antagonisms or in the *extravagances* of the ruling ideas we find there. It is precisely in this way we must account to ourselves for this war, or we shall not account for it satisfactorily at all—because no other method will give us the true and last solution of it.

Guided, then, by this preliminary statement, the first thing for us to do, in conducting the present investigation, is to interrogate the age we live in, and learn from it what are the mother principles that lie at the bottom of its society; what are the political phenomena to which they give birth; how and why disturbances grow out of them; what element is present in excess; and what ingredient is absent, and therefore needed to correct their vicious action. All this is not now difficult of ascertainment. History has obtained such a prolongation, and has accumulated such a mass of facts, which science has to some extent already classified, that it is capable of affording us all the satisfaction, derivable from induction and analogy, we can desire; and these methods, if properly employed, cannot fail to yield us such a solution of the problem in question as to give us at least a better insight into the nature of our difficulties than we had before. I shall not scruple, therefore, to appeal to history on every occasion where, in my opinion, any aid can be derived from its facts, or from the inductions which science has already extracted from them.

The filiation of the different epochs of history has been demonstrated by philosophers beyond dispute. Persons who have paid some attention to this branch of science will readily understand what is meant by the relationship of the ages; and those who have not, will excuse the omission here of any information on that subject; time and space will not allow the digression. Let it suffice to say, what indeed all well-informed persons know well enough, that the old theological *regime*, which lasted throughout the greater part of the middle ages—nearly a thousand years—held society benumbed during that long period in a theocratic form of government almost as pure as the old theocracies of the East. But that social condition, though it lasted long, could not endure forever; and the advent of the sixteenth century witnessed the beginning of its inevitable decay. Its advocates, however, deemed it to be eternal, because based, as they thought, on principles that were absolute; and they accordingly fought hard and long for its perpetuity—a battle which has lasted with little interruption to this day. But the dominion of that antiquated despotism, spite of occasional spasms, has passed away forever. It displaced a system still more ancient than itself; and now, in its turn, gave way to ideas of more modern date. It cannot return upon us. Unable to hold its own against the natural progress of intelligence, it will never again serve as a basis of government. We may as soon expect paganism to reassert successfully its claims to social dominion, as that Catholicism shall once more take possession of society and rule over it. Each has had its day, and the ideas of both are equally exhausted and effete.

It was to break up this old system that Protestantism was inaugurated; and the principles it employed for that purpose were identical with those that are known at this day as the dogmas of the democratic creed. Originally of a purely religious nature, these dogmas gradually acquired a mixed form; they were early adopted by metaphysics as weapons of great force in the conduct of its disquisitions; and finally, having crossed the Atlantic, in the zenith of their power, they assumed in this country, without losing their influence over metaphysics and religion, an exclusively political character, which they have borne ever since.

There *appears* to be a great diversity of political ideas striving in society, but in reality there are but two orders of such ideas, and both are stated in the above paragraph. From this statement it will be seen that one of these sets of ideas is but the negation of the other, and that it is the commingling of the two sets in different proportions which creates the apparent multiplicity.* One set is derived from the doctrines of the old theological and military system of the middle and feudal ages, and constitutes the *religious* state of social science; the other set is derived from the reformation which was begun in the sixteenth century for the destruction of the old system, and was adopted by metaphysics for its own enfranchisement. Issuing from Protestantism, and passing through a philosophical form, when this last order of ideas came to be applied to social affairs, it constituted and still constitutes what may be called the *metaphysical* state of politics. From the first of these two sets of ideas are derived all notions of *order* in the political world; from the second are derived all notions of *progress;* and as men are inclined for conservatism or amelioration, they arrange themselves under one or the other of the two banners. It is not my purpose to follow in detail the conflicts of these two forces, or to notice the monstrous alliances they have sometimes formed, but to come at once to a consideration of the *organic* capacity of the latter, and see if they are equal to their pretensions.

This investigation I think will discover to us that these sentiments, potent as they were in demolishing

* See Comte's Positive Philosophy.

the old theological system of the middle ages, have utterly failed to reorganize society upon a permanent basis derived from themselves. On the contrary, from the moment they entered the arena of politics, they attempted to suppress every other principle which they found already in possession of government; and as the latter refused to be thus unceremoniously expelled, the antagonisms of the two sets of ideas have kept European societies in a state of perpetual anarchy and transformation ever since. Where, on the other hand, they arrived first at the basis of government, and took possession of society, as in this country, they have barred the entrance to all other principles, and, being unchecked in their action, have run into such excesses that society can enjoy no peace at all for them.

The new doctrines, in giving rise to nearly all the political phenomena of modern times, have given also to the politics of the times their character of instability. They instantly put society in motion, and have kept it agoing ever since. In stirring it out of its theological slumber of ages, they had no place prepared for its repose, but hurried it along in a career of mutations that has not ceased to this hour. What else, indeed, but endless oscillations could be expected from principles that are essentially revolutionary? Revolution was the sole purpose of their inauguration. They were invoked expressly to eliminate a worn-out system that was no longer able to satisfy the social needs of humanity. To this end they were peculiarly well adapted, because they were the negation, the very opposites, the speculative antitheses of the exhausted ideas they were destined to combat; and they opened up to human action a boundless expanse of freedom, and to human intelligence an endless sphere of speculation—liberty without qualification, discussion without determination.

This work of expulsion they accomplished with fidelity and signal ability. All honor to them for their brave defense of human rights! But true to their mission of destruction, they will not understand their incapacity for reconstruction. Having battered down the walls of an antiquated *regime*, of a thousand years' standing, already tottering with age, they conceit themselves capable, single-handed, of rebuilding, in its stead, a society that shall combine order with progress and security with advancement. By giving the widest latitude to human liberty—restricting no principle, limiting no idea—asserting all their dogmas to be absolute and universal—they hope, by means of such a formula, to secure at the same time systematic regularity and a harmonious coherence of all the social elements into a recombination that shall establish conservatism and amelioration as co-ordinate conditions of modern civilization. Now, this is precisely what society wants. Both *order* and *progress* are indispensable conditions of modern civilization; and their co-ordination in the same system is the grand social problem and the grand social difficulty of the age. The solution of this problem is just what these principles cannot accomplish, although they pretend to be "the last hope of humanity;" and in order to realize this hope, men push them to their utmost extremity. Hence the futile efforts that are being everywhere made to harmonize incongruities by reagents that are themselves eminently disorganizing—principles that, however powerful they may be for segregation, have no force of cohesion.

THE FRENCH REVOLUTION.

France, unlike many of her cotemporaries, seems to have escaped entirely the treacherous stage of Protestantism, and to have passed at once from the Catholic to the revolutionary state; that is, from the old theologico-military system to that social condition in which the metaphysical state of politics predominates. A true daughter of Mother Church to the last moment, and having no quarrel with the Catholic Unity, to destroy which the new doctrines were instituted, she seems nevertheless to have illustrated, more thoroughly than any other nation, the nature of the democratic principles; and to have done so instantaneously, as if on purpose to test, by a single trial strain, their capacity alike for speed and for bottom, for action and for endurance.

It was in the French Revolution, which was begun about the end of the eighteenth century, that the democratic doctrines reached their culmination in Europe, and demonstrated their incapacity for social organization, when located by themselves at the foundation of government. Like a severe logician, that famous revolution drew from the democratic principles *a priori*, as it were, their remotest, their ultimate consequences: it actually exhausted them of all they contained of good or bad, and then passed on and abandoned them forever. If, therefore, any nation wish to know, without making the experiment for itself, what those principles are capable of in any of the social relations of life, it has but to interrogate the history of that epoch of French society to have its desires or curiosity satisfied.

The *Sans-Culottes* were perhaps the very best known types of the same class of persons to be anywhere found. It was precisely this class, everywhere, that was affranchised by the new political creed, and elevated to be the successors of the newly deposed hereditary legislators of the world. With the fiery zeal of their nation, and the ardor of new-born liberty, the *Sans-Culottes* seized the reins of government in France; and putting the democratic principles to their utmost speed, made them do at once all they could do. What the *Sans-Culottes* and the democratic doctrines did in France during the short period of the Revolution, the same classes and the same doctrines will do in other nations sooner or later.

It is to France, therefore, and to that epoch of her history, we must frequently go, in order to discover the true tendencies of the fundamental dogmas of our own government; for it is only there they have been already run out to their last consequences; and to those consequences they must inevitably go in this country, some time or other, if the same latitude be allowed them here. That they do actually enjoy the same latitude here, and are rapidly tending to similar results, the present war sufficiently attests; and these facts will be made still more manifest in the progress of this work.

Though the French Revolution may be said to have been the period of their highest intensification in Europe, the democratic dogmas have allowed few European societies to escape unharmed; all have shared a common disorganization, though in different degrees, and with various modifications. Nor have they yet entirely discontinued their activity there; it is only intermitted. The nations are still smouldering volcanoes;

and the fires of revolution may, at any moment, break out afresh in them. Beneath the heaving and troubled mist which veils the destinies of Europe, there yet lie hidden the same disorganizing principles which have so often shaken her to the center. Like the religion of an epoch, the democratic polity must be metamorphosed, must pass through a sort of metempsychosis, and reappear in a different and higher form before it can cease its disturbing influence. It must be absorbed by government, and crystallized, as it were, into institutions, with combinations so complex and intimate, and so regulated by law and so obedient to order, that its dogmas shall lose their character of individuality and appear only as the formula of organized order and justice.

THE AMERICAN REVOLUTION.

The United States, since it passed through the grand crisis of its first revolution, which gave it a national existence, has been too much preoccupied with the rapid progress of its material and moral grandeur to do more than warm in its bosom the disorganizing sentiments that were destined at a later day to upheave its society by the violence of their excesses. This nation may be called the child of the democratic doctrines, for they presided at its birth, stood by its cradle, and have been mainly active in shaping all the subsequent modifications of its political life, until it has become as it were a living embodiment of their spirit. It is the only state of modern times whose government is organized exclusively on the dogmas of that political faith; and its origin is of so recent a date that it had no antecedents to limit or to assault them. They alone were in possession of society here before the Revolution, and have retained it ever since.

The Roman Empire, when it was destroyed, left Europe strewed with the seeds or the wrecks of nations. Most European societies, therefore, at the present day, either grew out of those famous ruins, or were founded anterior to them. Their governments, gradually establishing themselves cotemporaneously with the rise of the theologico-military system of the middle ages, derived their principles partly at first as a bequest from the old Roman civilization; but in the end they became based mainly on the religious dogmas prevalent at that epoch. When, therefore, the new doctrines were started for the purpose of demolishing the ancient system, all the social perturbations that followed arose from the necessary antagonism of the old and new ideas. The old, indignant at their intrusion, not only assaulted the new, and strove to exclude them from any share of sovereignty; but, by opposing, limited their action; and thus preserved Europe from the ruin or the despotism that might have ensued from the excesses of the latter, if they had taken exclusive possession of society there as they did here.

Whatever may be the future course of events in the United States, no such combats have taken place here yet, because there are no opposing principles in the frame of this government; nor was there ever any prior organization to be destroyed or attacked. On the subject of democracy, the people of this country have hitherto been a unit: the popular mind is as completely subjugated to its dogmas as if there were no other principles in the world; and in the whole structure of this political organization there is not any force sufficient to limit the absolute tendencies of those dogmas; but they have taken entire possession of the social system, as of the popular mind, and reign there alone.

In European societies, on the contrary, there are theoretical opinions, monarchical opinions, aristocratic opinions, democratic opinions: these all cross and jostle, struggle, become interwoven, limit and modify each other. The inability of the various principles to exterminate one another has at last compelled each to endure the others, and to live in common. Each consents to have only that part of government which falls to its share; and to allow no encroachments or tyranny from the others.*

Thus, while the variety of elements of European civilization, which limit without destroying each other, has produced such liberty and order as exist there, the predominance of one principle here must produce despotism or dissolution. We find the tyrannies and rapid decay of all the ancient civilizations springing from precisely the same source. In India, all over Western Asia, in Egypt, where only one principle of civilization prevailed, there society was dominated by one exclusive power, which would bear with no other. The worst tyrannies with which history abounds are to be found in those countries. But *there* society endured; simplicity produced monotony; the country was not destroyed; but there was no progression; society remained torpid and inactive. In Greece, on the contrary, where, in some of the States, a democracy very similar to our

* See Guizot's History of Civilization in Europe.

own prevailed, there "the unity of the social principle led to a development of wonderful rapidity; no other people ever ran so brilliant a career in so short a time. But Greece had hardly become glorious, before she appeared worn out: her decline, if not so rapid as her rise, was strangely sudden. It seems as if the principle which called Greek civilization into life was exhausted. No other came to invigorate it or supply its place." The reader cannot help but observe the wonderful similarity between the phenomena of the ancient Greek civilization and our own. The same species of tyranny is to be found in both countries; the same rapid rise; and, so far as present appearances go, the same sudden decline. The parallel is complete in every particular; a turbulent democracy; the proscription of every principle of a contrary tendency; the deleterious influence of a set of pestilent demagogues; and apparently the same melancholy end.

The perturbations which are now distracting this society, and which are destined to rend it to pieces, have arisen, not from the conflicts of opposing principles, as in modern Europe, but from the dissolving tendencies of the democratic polity, as in ancient Greece. When, hereafter, other principles shall demand admission in the structure of government, a different order of conflicts will occur, because the new principles will not be allowed to take their places without opposition. The doctrines of the democratic creed, like the religious ideas of the theological epoch, are capable of yielding earnest convictions; they have already taken a deep hold of the popular heart in this country: hence the ruinous lengths to which they will be carried, the tenacity with which they will be adhered to, and the stubborn resistance they will offer to the introduction of other sentiments which threaten to contradict their absolute sovereignty.

But it is time we examine the democratic doctrines themselves *seriatim*, notice their application to the facts of our past history, follow their tendencies into the future, and see if they justify the character here given of them.

II. The Democratic Principles.

Regarding the democratic polity, then, in a more special view, we shall discover in it three fundamental dogmas, which have been mainly instrumental in producing some of the most important social phenomena of modern times. They are as follows: LIBERTY OF CONSCIENCE; POPULAR SOVEREIGNTY; EQUALITY. These three principles are so blended and so directly related —the two latter resulting immediately from the first— that it is difficult to treat them separately without tautology. Taken together, they constitute the *trinity* of the democratic faith—a tri-unity which, whether considered in its unity or tri-plicity, has revolutionized the moral world, has been the main element of all social disturbances in this country, and, as I expect to show, is directly or indirectly responsible for this war. Nor is it to the past alone, or to the present, that the ill effects of the principles under review are confined. They have by no means exhausted their capacity for mischief. The present war, huge evil as it is, is not the only form, nor perhaps the worst, under which they are likely to manifest their vicious tendencies. They are yet destined, through many long years of the future, to become the direful spring of woes unnumbered to this hapless nation, unless a provident forethought arrest at once their mad career.

It does not enter into the plan of this work to show how necessary or unavoidable was the exclusive substitution of the democratic principles at the basis of this government, at the time it was constructed. The circumstances peculiar to that epoch of history rendered inevitable their adoption, unattended, at least for a period, by other ideas that might hinder their action. And even now, as a prime element of modern society, they are indispensable. A legitimate product of the social evolution, their presence in all the social systems of the age is peremptorily demanded by the nature of modern civilization. A conspicuous element of human nature, they were obliged, at the proper time, to reappear in human civilization. A complete development of the latter would be impossible without them. Civilization can produce nothing but what pre-exists in humanity, and it is bound to reproduce whatever exists there, and to reproduce them in the same relations they are found there. Human nature is not a simple substance; it is complex, concrete, a compound, made up of many elements compacted together, and as such must project itself in its civilization. By the laws of growth, in the moral as in the physical world, these elements are not all brought forward together; but are developed gradually, one by one, and in different relations. Obstructions are always attended by shocks more or less violent: if insurmountable, by dissolution. The social system that cannot duplicate its original, is doomed to quick decay, as in Greece; or to a torpidity little better than death, as in the societies of the East.

The lapse of time and the progress of events here have so far altered the condition of things, that the democratic principles can no longer be trusted alone at the helm of state, without those checks and guards, those complements, those aids and assistants, which have always been found necessary defenses against despotism or anarchy. Society here has advanced with prodigious strides; the growth of the nation and its civilization has been more expeditious than ever before heard of in the history of empires, Greece not excepted; all the external conditions of the country have changed; the population has doubled itself ten times; the territory has been nearly trebled; and all the wants of a very advanced and complex civilization are pressing their satisfaction, while the government has remained stationary in the simple form of its original construction. The habiliments so well adapted to the size of the nation at its birth, are not equally well fitted to its present gigantic proportions. Its giant limbs are, in many places, bursting through the seams of its early integuments. The time is come for it to put off the small-clothes of infancy, and assume the *virilis toga* of manhood. This is the natural course of things. In making this change of garments, society need experience no more difficulty than other things; particularly in this country, the boast of whose social system is the "*facility of changing the structure of government*, whenever and as often as the society shall think there is anything in it to amend."

The rational and deliberative method of the adoption of our political system, occurring as it did at a period when the human mind was much less informed of the nature of social laws than it now is, would seem to augur well for the prospect of assembling another convention, similar to that which formed the old Federal Constitution, to take into consideration the modifications which the changes of time and circumstances have made it necessary to introduce in the structure of government. The people of this country have been so long familiarized, by previous habits, with the uses of such conventions, and so many modifications have been introduced by them into the constitutions of the several States, with little or no popular commotions, that no insurmountable difficulties need be anticipated in calling together another such convention, now in the very crisis of the nation's fate, in order to snatch it from the jaws of ruin.

With a view, therefore, to the opening of this discussion, and to a preparation of the public mind for the task before it, I shall confine myself, not to eulogies of the democratic principles, of which they have had enough, but to a disclosure of their unfitness, in their present absolute character, to be alone the conservators of a great society like this. If, then, I bring accusations against the democratic principles, considered in this light, it is without anger I do so; for it was doubtless necessary that, under the circumstances, they should have been first at the basis of government here, and, for a period, to have been there alone. The time needed for their solitary development, I can well believe, could not have been abbreviated, nor the damage they have wrought avoided. It is not their fault if, like all human dogmas when spoilt by indulgence, they are capricious and extravagant, as well as intolerant and proscriptive. This war will not have been too dearly bought, if it be the occasion of correcting these defects, and of rectifying the error in the form of government which brought it about.

LIBERTY OF CONSCIENCE.

The necessity of a rapid *synthesis*, in the treatment of my subject, would seem almost to preclude the possibility of *analysis*, without too much diffuseness. The latter method, however, alone supplies the requisite amount of clearness. I shall, therefore, proceed to decompose the democratic polity into its several parts, and treat each part separately, even though it be at the risk of frequent repetitions and consequent tedium.

Of the three dogmas, included in the democratic trinity, mentioned above, the first is much the most important, both on account of its intrinsic value, and because it was the first great weapon so successfully employed by Protestantism against its powerful adversary, who claimed to be the keeper of all consciences, and allowed no freedom of opinion on the most vital concerns of this world or the world to come. It also set free the other two, made their acknowledgment a necessary consequence of its own, and imparts to them its own virtues and vices.

It is a singular fact, if true,—and M. Guizot seems to have demonstrated its truth, satisfactorily at least to his own mind,—that the Catholic Church itself was the first to liberate this principle at a very early period of its history. It was about the beginning of the fifth century that the Church was obliged to declare a separation of temporal and spiritual authority, in order to defend itself against the brute force of the times. This separation is, in the opinion of M. Guizot, the only true source of liberty of conscience. The separation, according to him, was based upon no other principle than that which serves as the groundwork of the strictest and most extensive liberty of conscience. The separation of temporal and spiritual power, he says, rests solely upon the idea that physical force has no authority over the mind, over convictions, over truth; so that, however paradoxical it may seem, that very principle of liberty of conscience for which Europe has so long struggled against the whole power of the Church, for which it has suffered so much, which has only so lately prevailed, and that against the will of the clergy—that very principle was acted upon, under the name of a separation of the temporal and spiritual power, in the infancy of European civilization. It was, moreover, the Christian Church itself that introduced and maintained it, when driven to assert it by the circumstances in which it was placed, as a means of defense against barbarism.

In all this, far-fetched as it is, M. Guizot would seem to be the mere apologist of the Church; or perhaps he would thereby lay claim to a degree of penetration or philosophical acumen in his historical researches which no other author ever possessed, for it is the first time liberty of conscience was ever heard of as a constituent element of society at that early epoch. In claiming liberty of conscience as a permanent benefit conferred by Catholicism on European society as early as the fifth century, M. Guizot convicts that arbitrary power of an inconsistency not a whit better than the tyranny which its continuous suppression would imply; for it is very certain that, when the barbarians were conquered, and all the other elements of society were reduced to a state of subordination to the authority of the Catholic Church, that despotic *regime* closed the mind of society against the principle of liberty of conscience, and kept it effectually so closed for the long period of nearly a thousand years. When, subsequently, the human intelligence revolted against this despotism, and claimed liberty of conscience as an indefeasible right, the Catholic unity fought against it with all its might. This fact, however, does not convict M. Guizot of error, for it is not a solitary instance of inconsistency on the part of the Catholic Church. In Protestant countries, even at this day, it clamors as loudly as any for liberty of conscience; while in Catholic nations the same right is systematically proscribed. Thus we see the Catholics in England, and yet more in Ireland, asserting the claim of liberty of conscience, while still calling loudly for the repression of Protestantism in France, Austria, and elsewhere.*

The error of M. Guizot lies more on the surface of his statement, which I cannot stop here to point out. To me, the opinion—for it is nothing but an opinion—seems to be more a piece of sportive fancy than a matter of fact, an unauthorized inference drawn from an historical incident, a forced construction of an event which did actually take place. It is very clear the Catholic

* See Comte's Positive Philosophy.

Church never thought of liberating anybody's conscience; it only thought of its own interests, and how it might defraud or coerce the barbarian. Liberty of conscience was a thing then unknown in the world. Society at that period would have known as little what to do with liberty of conscience as the human mind at this day would know how to do without it. It was due to M. Guizot's high standing as an author, and to the prominent place this opinion occupies in the ablest of his works, to record it here, which I do simply for what it is worth.

M. Comte, in my opinion, was much nearer the truth in the assertion that, when the dogma of liberty of conscience was proclaimed, for the first time, in the sixteenth century, as a revolutionary principle, to release the nations from the tyranny of the theological *regime*, the impulse of the emancipation was irresistible; and the revolutionary contagion was, in this one respect, universal. It attracted to its standard all orders of minds, from the highest to the lowest, and continues to this day a chief characteristic of the mind of society.

From having at first a purely religious application, liberty of conscience soon passed into a favorite political dogma; and in this country it has established itself, with its two co-ordinate principles, exclusively at the foundation of our social system. Its domination of society here is supreme, and the popular mind, in all its operations, acknowledges no other stimulant. Nor is there a single contradictory principle admitted in the frame of our society sufficient to limit its authority. The wildest vagaries, and the greatest possible divergencies of opinions, must be the first necessary consequences of this unrestricted sovereignty of a single, unopposed principle; and, in the long run, a despotism, not inferior to that of the Catholic unity in the middle ages, will result from the democratic unity in this country. Between anarchy and despotism there is perhaps little choice; and the perpetual vibration of society between those two extremes, with unsatisfactory revolutions to fill up the intervals, presents to us a future fraught with horrors enough to appal the stoutest heart. Such, however, under the patronage of this lawless dogma, must be our alternatives, unless rescued by an intelligent patriotism and a wise provision.

It is a law of physics that the tendency of every force is to excess. In natural systems, this tendency is counteracted by the limitation of one force by another, and a due equipoise is obtained by the development from the forces themselves of a regular system of checks and balances. In social arrangements, which are always more or less artificial, this prudent limitation of principles is not always observed. The metaphysical habitude of the general mind, so prevalent in this age, favors *absolute* views, to the almost utter exclusion of *relative* notions. This dangerous mental habit, not yet counteracted by the advance of positive science, was first introduced into Europe, along with Protestantism, in the sixteenth century. It is the legitimate successor of the theological method of disquisition, and was engendered partly by the ignorance of natural laws, but mainly by the freedom of inquiry which followed the introduction of liberty of conscience. From Europe it was transported, in the plenitude of its power, to this country; and from being an exotic, it soon became naturalized, and took such deep root in the popular mind that it has ever since rather improved than declined. Thus nationalized, it is a powerful ally of liberty of conscience, and by its method of discussion renders that licentious dogma more dangerous than it would otherwise be. In the discussion of nearly all questions, therefore, under favor of this metaphysical habit, the necessary stimulant of the mind, as in theology, is the *infinite;* for every debater professes himself to be a philosopher, that is, a metaphysician, who thinks nothing of penetrating to the essence of things and to ultimate causes, and seeks habitually for the most latitudinous construction of ideas. Under such conditions, a principle, to be good for anything at all, must be able to bear every strain that can be put on it, and be run out to endless consequences, without limitations from any quarter.

A fit illustration of this tendency is afforded by the revisions which the constitutions of most of the States have undergone within the last quarter of a century. Many of the States had constitutions in which it was thought the democratic polity was too much restricted; it was still further to *democratize* or *popularize* them that conventions were assembled for their revision. In some States this had to be done more than once within a very short period before democracy could be satisfied. It was argued by the metaphysical politicians that democracy, if good for anything, must be good for everything pertaining to government; that if the people be capable of electing one set of officers, they were equally capable of electing all; of sitting in judgment on all political questions; and of solving every social problem that could occupy the attention of the human mind.

This argument exactly suited the people; it accordingly prevailed; and constitutions were formed, in which the democratic principles were left, like eternity, without limits. Democracy now culminated; every branch of government was in its hands—the legislative, the executive, the judiciary; its unity was complete; its domination of society absolute.

By this same metaphysical habit of mind, so dangerous when used by incompetent persons, a boundless application is given to the principle of liberty of conscience. It is made to carry itself into all the practical details of social life, and to cover a multitude of human rights. Some of the most important of these rights are—the right of free inquiry, the right of every man to his own opinions, the right of speech, and of every other mode of expression by which opinions can be communicated. Now, if it were true, as democracy claims, that all men are equal,—equally wise, equally just, equally virtuous and good, and those qualities were absolute and unlimited in all men,—in that case there would be no necessity for government or laws; every man would be a law unto himself, and order and progress would prevail spontaneously. That is the sole condition under which those rights can be conceded; and I leave it to every one to determine for himself if that condition exists.

That no one may be shocked at this novel appreciation of the dogma of free inquiry, or liberty of conscience, it will be necessary to examine more closely some of the consequences likely to flow from the immense aggrandizement claimed for it, and point out its legitimate limits; for, be it remembered, there is nothing in this world that is absolute and unlimited: all things sublunary are relative merely, all have their qualifications, their metes and bounds; and it is the duty of government to define these, and establish them, in all matters of social concernment.

This formula, then, regarded as absolute,—for it is really in that light it is considered in this country,—abolishes everything like *intellectual regulations*, and sets up the personal reason as supreme authority in all notions that can engage the attention of the human understanding. There are, accordingly, in this country no less than thirty millions of supreme authorities in all the moral, intellectual, and social concerns of life. Each of these arbiters decides from the tribunal of his own conscience; and from this authority there is no appeal. Each is entitled to the broadest liberty of inquiry and to endless discussion; and his opinions, when formed, however wrong they may be, are sacred, for there is for him no other standard of right but his own conscience. Here, then, is reached a point of intellectual dissipation which upsets all fixed principles of action, where unity of thought is in danger of being lost in a ruinous diversity, and which renders government next to an impossibility.

I have already said that the natural tendency of everything is to excess, and it is in their extremities that all things find their ruin. To this vicious tendency the human mind is peculiarly exposed; and there are few opinions which, if unrestricted, do not proceed to the full length of their tethers. In the exercise of its functions, the human intelligence is apt, like everything else, when a momentum is given to it in a certain direction, to rush beyond the safe limits of that middle term where a due equilibrium resides, and to go to the verge of dissolution. As society follows the lead of intelligence, and symbolizes its speculations, this tendency of the human mind constitutes the greatest danger to which the former is exposed, for it represents a state of dissipation little short of absolute anarchy. Inasmuch, therefore, as every government is based on sentiments which it is bound to reproduce in its phenomena, the government of this country is of course no exception to that rule. On the contrary, as a perfect reflex of the democratic polity and a faithful exponent of all its dogmas, the government of the United States, in the administration of public affairs, has frequently run into the excesses authorized by the sentiments contained in the dogma of liberty of conscience. The examples thus set in high quarters have not wanted followers in lower spheres: they have descended to the administrations of State governments, to the most minute ramifications of general and special politics, and to private practices as well. I shall mention but two or three of these instances, as samples of all. These examples I shall take from the most exalted sources—sources which, on account of their altitude, not only entitle them to attention, but render them peculiarly noticeable and exposed to observation.

The first of these illustrations which I shall mention is drawn from the administration of General Jackson, in 1832, when democracy culminated in the Federal government. That distinguished personage, in his celebrated Message vetoing the bill for the recharter of the United States Bank, used the following language:—

"Each public officer who takes an oath to support the constitution, swears that he will support it *as he understands it*, and not as it is understood by others." This sentiment influenced his vetoes of several important bills, on constitutional grounds *as he understood them.* The consequence was that many of his vetoes and other official acts were in direct opposition to precedents, to long-established usages, to the practices of all anterior administrations, extending through more than forty years; they were also opposed to decisions of the highest judicial tribunal of the land, appointed exclusively to sit in judgment on constitutional questions.

It cannot but be seen, at first view, that a general adoption of this sentiment as a universally received political maxim of binding force, would dissolve government and render social order wholly impracticable. Nevertheless, the sentiment was in strict accordance with the spirit of the age and government, of which General Jackson, as its organ, was a faithful exponent. There were, however, even at that epoch, minds sufficiently exempt from the lawless domination of that spirit to characterize such a sentiment as it deserved. In an able speech, delivered in the Senate of the United States, Mr. Webster unmasked the insidious danger that lurked beneath its specious exterior. Commenting on this text, he very justly remarked that it would raise every man's private opinions into a standard for his own conduct; and of course there can be no government where every man is to judge for himself of his own rights and his own obligations. Where every one is his own arbiter, force, and not law, is the governing power. He who may judge for himself, and decide for himself, must execute his own decisions; and this is the law of force. If he, who is appointed to *execute* the laws, has the right to interpret them for himself, then also has he, whose only duty is to *obey* the laws, the same right. And where all men enjoy this privilege, and each is entitled to obey the laws only according to his own understanding of them, there is an end to all constitutional and legal restrictions. Such a sentiment abolishes the judiciary, and abrogates the obligations of the whole criminal code. Culprits would have to be tried, not according to the law, but according *as they profess to understand it.* Arguments would have to be addressed, and appeals made, not to a bench of judges or a box of jurors, but to the accused themselves, in order to enlighten them how they ought to understand the law.

The next example which I shall cite is taken, not like the other from the official acts of the Federal administration, but from the legislative acts of one of the State governments. Both are so eminent in their origin, and so notorious as events of history, that they are in no danger of being perverted or misrepresented without detection. About the same time, then, that General Jackson, as Chief Magistrate of the United States, uttered the above sentiment, that is, in 1832, the Legislature of South Carolina so far followed the example and adopted the maxim of the "Old Chief" as to nullify a law of Congress, on the ground, *they said*, that it was not warranted by the Federal Constitution *as they understood that instrument.* Such, in the last analysis, was the true origin of the famous South Carolina Ordinance of Nullification, which came so near dissolving the Union more than thirty years ago; although Mr. Calhoun professed to derive his precedent, not from General Jackson or the Federal administration, but from Mr. Jefferson, who, in the Virginia and Kentucky Resolutions of 1798–9, uttered, in effect, precisely the same sentiment as that quoted from General Jackson's Veto Message. This act of South Carolina, perpetrated *avowedly* on the ground that each State possessed the right of interpreting the constitution and laws of Congress *as she understood them*, and of nullifying the latter whenever, *in her opinion*, they conflicted with the former, constituted the most perilous moment, prior to 1861, which ever occurred in the history of this government. That the danger was fully understood, even at that early period; that it was even then attributed to the proper source; that the doctrine of General Jackson's Veto Message and the Nullification Ordinance of South Carolina were directly related and owned a common origin; and that I draw no unauthorized inference from either, are all made clearly manifest by speeches delivered at that time in the Senate Chamber of the United States by the most distinguished orators and statesmen of that day. In proof of this I shall make a few extracts from a speech of Mr. Webster, who, with the prescience of true greatness, looking far ahead of ordinary minds, exclaimed: "*Are we not threatened with dissolution of the Union?* Are we not told that the laws of the government shall be openly and directly resisted? At this moment, so full of peril to the State, the Chief Magistrate puts forth opinions as truly subversive of all government as the wildest theories of nullification. There is not an individual in its ranks, capable of putting two ideas together, who, if you grant him the principles of the Veto Message, cannot defend all that nullification has ever threatened." "The President of the United States is of opinion, that an individual, called on to execute a law, may himself judge of its constitutional validity. Does nullification teach anything more revolutionary than that? The President is of opinion, that every officer is bound to support the constitution only according to what ought to be, in his private opinion, its construction. Has nullification, in its wildest flight, reached to an extravagance beyond that? The President is of opinion, that judicial interpretations of the constitution and laws do not bind the consciences, and ought not to bind the conduct, of men. Is nullification at all more disorganizing than that?" "Nullification, it is in vain to deny it, is dissolution; it is dismemberment; it is the breaking up of the Union," etc.

Such, then, were the opinions, such the apprehensions, of the most practical statesman of his day, as to the dangerous direction of public affairs, and as to the safety of the Union itself, under the patronage of this licentious doctrine. Without, perhaps, penetrating to its last cause, to the true source of its origin, Mr. Webster yet saw, or rather *felt*, in a moment of prophetic frenzy peculiar to highly endowed minds, that a sentiment so disorganizing as that uttered by the then head of the Federal government, and practically illustrated by one of the States, must ultimately terminate in brute force and dissolution of the Union.

At that early period, abolitionism, as a party cry, was unheard of; the negro question, as a disturbing element of society, occasioned no uneasiness; the abolition of slavery was a private sentiment only, which had not yet passed beyond the precincts of a few individual minds; and no one, perhaps, dreamed that it ever would become the rallying note of a great party destined to the bad ends which it has apparently contributed so much to accomplish. All those secondary causes, which are now convulsing the nation, were then in abeyance, or, at most, merely rudimental; and yet a social cataclysm exactly analogous to the present was already imminent, and was averted mainly because society was not then fully ripe for the catastrophe. Nevertheless, it is plain that the two sets of causes, those of 1832 and those of 1861, both secondary in their natures, and however different they may be in appearance, sprang from the same source; they were the offsprings of the same parent; and, possessing the same disorganizing qualities, tended of course to similar consequences. This common origin is not difficult to discover: it is to be found in the dogma of liberty of conscience, the fruitful parent of so much licentiousness both of theory and practice.

One other illustration will serve to render this fact still more clear, and, at the same time, to mark the progress which the dogma of liberty of conscience and its co-ordinate rights had made in a comparatively short time in demoralizing the mind of society and preparing it for final dissolution.

This, then, brings us to the third and last example which I shall cite. The extraordinary sentiment, quoted above, emanating from the then Chief Magistrate of the nation, and appearing in an important state paper as a fundamental maxim of his administration, and subsequently reduced to practice by a State government, was timid and hesitating. It did not go the length of denying the paramount authority of constitutions and laws: it acknowledged their supremacy, but dissipated their binding force by referring their construction to individual understandings. At a later period, we hear accredited to another high public functionary, then a United States Senator, now a cabinet minister, a sentiment of similar import, but which so far transcends the other as to set aside altogether legislative enactments in favor of a "higher law," which is paramount to all constitutions, and which, when the two come in conflict, is alone binding on the consciences and conduct of men. What this "higher law" is, whence it emanates, from whom it derives its authority, how it is to be enforced, or what are its guarantees, we are not exactly told. It appears to be some unwritten law of God or of Nature, which every one must interpret for himself. Or rather, it seems to be a dictate of every man's own conscience, which he is under a moral obligation to obey in preference to any municipal law whatever. Or, in short, it is difficult to say what it is, or how many there are; for the phrase "higher *law*" appears to be a noun of multitude, a sort of generic term, which covers an indefinite number of laws. This sentiment, vague as it is, made such progress as to obtain currency with a party which became a prime element in dissolving the Union, and which is even now controlling the government of the nation, and conducting the war in a manner which does not pretend to be constitutional, but in open defiance of the constitution.

To superficial observers, these "sayings and doings" may well seem trivial, and attract little attention as signs of the times. Standing alone as isolated sentiments of the individuals uttering them, they were, perhaps, thought to be intellectual extravagances, exuberances of mind, which were never intended to pass beyond their verbal expression: and few persons are able to connect their acts as links in the great chain of events, and deduce from them the direction of history. Even nullification, significant as was that great event, yielded no lesson on this subject. It was thought to be a mere ebullition of the moment, a temporary disturbance, having no connection with the past and no reference to the future. Its true genealogy seems never to have been suspected. It was deemed to have been called suddenly into being by the Tariff Act of 1828, and as suddenly allayed forever by the Compromise Bill of Mr. Clay. But all these sentiments and acts, these "sayings and doings," trivial and isolated as they may seem at first sight, are legitimate derivatives of liberty of conscience and its co-ordinate rights. These lawless rights, so boundless in their pretensions, are genuine revolutionary principles. They have already demolished an ancient system cemented by the prescription of a thousand years. The theological *regime* of the middle ages dissolved at their touch. The military system of feudalism fell before them. In pure wantonness, they would seem to have constructed a sort of "card-house" government here, for apparently no other purpose than to gratify their disorganizing instincts by demolishing it at a single blow as soon as erected. If they succeed in reconstructing it, it will be only to level it once more to the ground with a breath as before. They have so long controlled public and private opinions in this country, that they have at last passed into the commonest truisms, the merest matters of course, which it is considered a species of insanity to question. Their very commonness, their nearness to us, and the close intimacy they have formed with our every-day thoughts, render them in a manner invisible. Their destructive agency is the last thing to be suspected. In seeking for the cause of our troubles, we *overlook* them altogether. We accuse first one thing and then another. Symptoms are mistaken for diseases; occasions for causes. The sad experience we are now undergoing ought to be a convincing and long-remembered preacher on this subject, and teach us to look nearer home for the source of our misfortunes; to look for it in our own hearts, in our own minds, in the bosom of our social system, for it is only there we can come at the real root of the evil.

Everything has a reason for existing—its necessity, its utility, its law. Some such latitude of discussion as is authorized by this vagabond liberty of conscience, was needed to combat successfully the crushing weight of authority exercised by the religious government of the Catholic Church in its long day of power; and liberty of conscience correctly represents the state of unbounded freedom in which the human mind was left by the decay of the old theological *regime.* It has also not been without its utility in enabling philosophers to explore the entire field of thought; and, by admitting the right of all to a similar research, encouraged the discussion which must precede and effect the discovery of principles which will solicit a new social organization that shall combine order with progress; and which, while it neglects not the interests of society, neither will it slight the development of the individual. Herein alone consist the necessity and utility of this release of the human mind from the old authority. Liberty of conscience correctly represents that enfranchisement. Its business was to tear down the old system, to clear the ground and prepare the materials for a reorganization of society. For this purpose it was necessary that it should exercise all the prerogatives of an *absolute* principle; otherwise it is clear it never could have possessed the requisite amount of energy to accomplish its revolutionary mission.

With the fulfillment of that object, its dangerous activity ought to have ceased. The very freedom of inquiry which it authorized ought long ago to have detected the imposition it so successfully practiced in passing itself off for an *absolute* principle; and with the detection and exposure of this imposition, its further interference with the reorganization of society would have been confined within salutary bounds. But such was very far from being the case. Once put in motion it seems not to know where to stop. Released from the trammels of ages, and started on a mission of the highest importance to the interests of humanity, its first successes have only magnified its zeal; and, with the accomplishment of its original purpose, instead of diminishing its efforts, it seems rather to have gained strength ever since. Its activity no longer absorbed by the demolition of the old political order, it now aims at an entire reorganization of society on a basis of its own. But the right of free inquiry is of so dissolving a nature that it never can become an organic principle. On the contrary, every attempt it makes to reconstruct a permanent system of government must prove disastrous to the age or nation that allows the experiment. Witness the example of Mexico, of the Central and South American Republics, the Italian Republics, the short episode of the French Republic. Witness, finally, and above all, the brilliant illustration which this country is just now adding to other examples of failure of the democratic experiment.

Such a principle as the right of unbounded liberty of conscience, and the collateral rights that flow from it, can never produce anything else but simple *individual* thoughts. The thoughts thus produced must be as diverse as the characters of the thinkers, with no common center of attraction stronger than the mere *wills* of those who entertain them. Possessing, then, no principle of convergence other than the caprices of countless individual minds, accustomed, in the respect of their opinions, to the wildest license, these vagrant sentiments must owe to the *voluntary* assent of numbers whatever supremacy they can ever possess. And such, indeed, is the only method of procuring the famous "*majority*" so much vaunted in this country. The decisions which issue from this judgment-seat of the populace really establish nothing at all; for the questions decided by it remain still open, and the discussion may be renewed again and again, *ad infinitum*, without any definitive settlement ever being arrived at. Where the right of inquiry is never closed, and the whims of licentious minds is the only law employed to solicit a unanimity of sentiments, the *majority* is liable to shift from side to side, and to vary its decisions so often, that distraction, and not settlement, will be the consequence. If anything was wanting to realize, in its worst form, a diversity of so dissolving a nature, and to render it in practice as ruinous as it appears in theory, this end was obtained in the *frequency* of elections established by law in this country, and the admission as voters of all male white persons above the age of twenty-one years.

In point of fact, the unbounded right of free inquiry *imposes the necessity of never deciding.* From this state of prolonged indecision ensues an irritation of the public mind, which in time becomes intolerable. Our whole government is a practical illustration of this melancholy fact. From its commencement to the present moment, not a single question of importance, although so often referred to the arbitration of the *majority*, and debated *ad nauseam*, has ever been determined. All the Presidential elections of the last thirty years have vibrated, like a pendulum, from one side to the other of these great questions. Take, for example, the elections of Messrs. Adams, Jackson, Van Buren, Harrison, Polk, Taylor, Pierce. In each of these elections the main questions to be decided were precisely the same; and each decision was a direct reversal of its predecessor. After seven verdicts of the majority, each, with a solitary exception, annulling the other and reaffirming itself, the policy of the government was left as indeterminate at last as at first. Four years after Mr. Pierce's term, a new party came into power, complicating without displacing the old issues, and rendering a final judgment on any of them that much more difficult and distant. Thus nearly forty years were consumed in earnest but futile efforts to establish a fixed rule of action to guide the administration of public affairs in certain matters considered to be of vital importance to the nation.

After these reiterated trials, nothing seemed more improbable than that a satisfactory conclusion would ever be reached by this method of adjustment; and nothing seemed more likely than that the majority should continue, as heretofore, to shift from side to side to the end of the chapter. And yet it was impossible, in the nature of things, that this state of indecision should last forever. Such a condition was opposed to the constitution of the human mind. The suspense had already extended beyond the average duration of human lifetime; and instead of improving, it was continually growing worse and worse. If the patience of one of the parties had not broke down under the last complication, there is no telling to what additional excesses the public mind might have gone. As it is, the nation, at this moment, is a fit emblem of the utter confusion its political dogmas are so well calculated to produce. This or a similar climax was the inevitable consequence of those dogmas. It might have been longer delayed, or it might have happened sooner; but, sooner or later, some such catastrophe was bound to be brought about by the very terms of our political system.

If it were possible for discussion to produce decision, our social policy would have been settled long ago, and society would have remained tranquil to this day. The greatest possible freedom of inquiry and the widest latitude of discussion were allowed and indulged during the election campaigns mentioned above. Every conceivable method of investigation was employed. The country was "stumped" from one end to the other. The highest order of eloquence resounded over the land. The lowest "clap-traps" in the way of oratory were not wanting.

Thousands of political newspapers, consecrated to the sole purpose of influencing the vote of the majority, helped to swell the monstrous inquisition. Nothing, in short, that was likely to cause conviction, or persuasion, or deception, was left untried. It will reside in the memory of all who participated in those notorious campaigns, how boisterous and stormy they were. Their violence, engendered by licentiousness, not liberty, shook the nation to its center. Few governments on the earth could have withstood such shocks. But, as yet, the conservative spirit of the people was stronger than the disorganizing tendency of their social principles. Nevertheless, as they swept over the land with their stormy debates, they deposited the seeds of future crops of whirlwinds, to be afterward reaped in kind, the first of which we are now harvesting with blood and tears.

To say that a perpetual discussion of the foundations of society is consistent with social order, is to reverse the well-known conditions of human nature, and to place the repose of humanity in endless strife and confusion. No amount of intelligence in the people can render such an arrangement compatible with that equilibrium which it is the design of society to secure; and where that intelligence rates low in the scale of intellectual development, the disturbance must be proportionably great. So long as there is no standard of right but the individual conscience, and no authority that speaks with the voice of command, closing debate peremptorily by pronouncing judgments that shall be final, society must be abandoned to the caprices of opinions as divergent as the eccentricities of the human intelligence will allow them to be. This state of indecision, with no fixed points of conviction, must in time beget in the public mind a kind of morbid perturbation that cannot be prolonged beyond a certain point without serious danger. We ignore the deepest necessities of human reason when we deny to it the repose it seeks in decisions that are irreversible. When the repose of society is dependent on the same conditions, how is it conceivable that rational men will intrust the stability of government and the security of social rights to no firmer basis than that afforded by this arbitrary principle? We would esteem him a madman who should resolve and re-resolve, from day to day, without ever coming to a definite conclusion on anything. If, therefore, it be reckoned madness in an individual to be always examining and never deciding, assuredly no dogmatic consecration of such conduct in the aggregate of individuals or in society can constitute the perfection of social order. The mental irritation consequent on the adjournment of important questions to readjudications without end, must at last produce such a sense of desperation that one party or the other would be constrained to appeal to the arbitrament of the sword, as a *dernier ressort;* and if the arrangement could be imagined permanent, brute force would once more, as of old, sit umpire over the world, and progress retrace its steps to the camps of Attila and Gengis Khan.

The political annals of our country afford an apt illustration of the truth of this argument. All the Presidential elections anterior to that of 1860 were decisions of the majority, affirming and reaffirming the constitutional guarantees and the policy of the government on the subject of slavery, and adjudging to the South the undisturbed enjoyment of its peculiar institution. The election of Mr. Lincoln was deemed at last to have reversed all those prior decisions, and to have imperiled the social rights of the South. For long years before, the mental irritation of the Southern people, caused by a knowledge of the instability of those popular decisions, and by the threatening aspect of the fickle multitude at the North, had already become chronic. The knowledge that, at any moment, their dearest rights were liable to be taken from them by an irresponsible majority that professed allegiance to a higher law than human constitutions, left them no choice as to what their conduct should be in the event of their worst fears being realized. That point, where patience ceased to be a virtue, was deemed to have been reached by the election of Mr. Lincoln. The binding force of the constitution, weakened by the right of individual constructions, had ceased to afford any sense of security. The popular mind, debauched by licentious dogmas and by loose sentiments deduced from them, was ripe for any disturbance. The morbid perturbation of Southern society, so long kept up by all these causes, broke out into open revolt at the first and flimsiest pretext that came to hand, and the present war ensued.

Here the dogma of

POPULAR SOVEREIGNTY

suggests itself, as growing so directly out of the right of free inquiry, or liberty of conscience, that the latter cannot be treated further without mixing up the former with it. Free inquiry, or liberty of conscience, considered as absolute, assigns to every one the right of sitting in judgment on all social questions whatever; and the doctrine of universal suffrage, as practiced in this country, actually consigns those delicate questions, in effect, *exclusively* to the least cultivated understandings of the nation's entire population. For the mass of population in any country necessarily consists of that class of persons; and where universal suffrage obtains, the *majority*, which decides all political questions, must contain the least informed minds as the principal element of its composition.

It is universally conceded that social problems are, of all others, the most complex and the most difficult of solution. For ages they have challenged the attention of the best minds, and, like distant *nebulæ*, have hitherto defied the highest powers of the human intelligence to resolve them. None have so much claim to be consigned to the choicest intellects which shall have been highly prepared for the investigation of questions so obscure and so mixed up with human passions. It would seem, then, scarcely consistent with good sense or sound policy to turn over these subtle questions to the decisions of persons who have never received any intellectual training, and the minds of many of whom are almost brutalized by ignorance. Yet the dogma of popular sovereignty proposes nothing less; and, in the case of this country, we actually witness the remarkable phenomenon of the government of one of the largest nations on the earth delivered into the hands of the most ignorant portion of thirty millions of population. The political formula that "the majority shall rule," actually accomplishes this anomaly. It condemns all the superior to an arbitrary dependence on the multitude of the inferior; and it transfers to the people, to the ignorant masses, the divine right to govern, which has long been the opprobrium of kings.

I do not assert too much when I say that the majority always consists of the most ignorant and inferior portion of a nation's population. This is necessarily the case. However many degrees of difference there may be, morally and intellectually, between the individuals composing the majority, it is evident they belong not to the *choice few*, who alone are fitted, by a high natural organization and previous preparation, to deal with problems so intricate as those upon which society is based. It is well known that a very large majority of the inhabitants of all nations belongs to what is called the *masses*—the *rudis indigestaque moles humani*—a phrase which admirably describes those persons who, however excellent and useful they may be in their places, yet, looked at from an intellectual point of view, would scarcely realize one's *beau ideal* of eminent statesmen and legislators. With, comparatively speaking, low mental and moral organizations, their physical endowments and exclusively physical training adapt them to the material drudgeries of life, and to those laborious but necessary offices which they perform so well. Incapacitated by nature for high intellectual developments, even if their time and means allowed the experiment, which they do not, it is only routine duties they can discharge in the great social hives of humanity. The economy of nature has assigned their place in society. No artifice can better the arrangement. In all ages they have been the *mutes* in the great drama of the

Social Evolution, and have passed over the stage of history in dumb show, without word or speech, knowing the meaning of nothing that goes on. The *vis inertia* of a nation's population, they are blind instruments in the hands of others, and are always to be dreaded when taken out of their places and set in motion on political occasions.

Whether it was originally intended for earnest or jest, it is certain that the celebrated apothegm of *vox populi, vox Dei,* contains the bitterest irony that ever was uttered, to say nothing of its impiety. It has long been a favorite text of Fourth-of-July declamation, and has no doubt deceived many silly minds. But, notwithstanding this consecration of the popular voice, there is no instance on record where ever God delivered his oracles by the multitude, or nature truths by the herd. Though there are many examples recorded of individual men having been called to these divine missions, and all the great benefits which have, at divers times, been conferred on society, have originated, so far as we know, from single minds, the masses, on the contrary, have ever been an element of social disturbances; and wherever they have appeared conspicuously on the field of politics, social cataclysms of one kind or other have invariably followed. If, therefore, the people have ever been employed as agents in the hands of God for any purpose whatever, it has been as instruments of his vengeful, not of his beneficent providences; and there have been few societies in the world which have not experienced, at one time or other, this evidence of the divine displeasure. While history abounds with evidences of the people's unfitness to be a dominant element in any social system, it affords not a single instance to the contrary. *Vox populi, vox diaboli,* therefore, would be a much more appropriate aphorism than the other.

It is to the arbitrary and variable decisions of a multitude so incompetent that the doctrine of popular sovereignty abandons all social questions whatever. Now, imagine ideas, upon which depends the very existence of society, consigned, not for one time only but for all time, to a heterogeneous mass like this: is it conceivable that any government could resist forever the dissolving action of so much diversity, and of such corrosive discussion as is authorized by the dogma of free inquiry? So far from it, all true social order is incompatible with the vagabond liberty of individual minds here implied. If such license were to last, a dissolution of the social state must ensue, through the ever-growing divergence of individual understandings. We all know the kind of frenzy that seizes the popular mind on occasions of important political elections; how little of reason, and how much of passion, sways the deliberations of the people; and how completely their individual understandings are delivered over to their disorderly impulses, and to the impurest of motives. Now, is it probable that, under these circumstances, ideas, upon which depends the safety of society, and which are of all others the most easily perverted, are likely to receive the best interpretations of which they are susceptible?

To these objections it may be replied, that the government of this country, erected upon the polity here arraigned, has so far procured order and progress that society, under its protection, has developed in an unprecedented manner, and that no element of true greatness in the life of a nation has been neglected, but all have advanced *pari passu*, within an incredibly short time, to the highest eminence ever reached in the oldest nations.

This is true. It would be a waste of time to enumerate all the causes that have been most active in procuring such extraordinary results: they are patent to every mind that has paid the least attention to the history of the times. The social marvels we have witnessed have been brought about, not in consequence of the democratic polity, but in spite of it. All other conditions remaining the same, similar results might have been procured under an Oriental despotism. The country was so young, so fresh, so vigorous, that it was able to bear a great deal of bad government, even if such had existed; but, in point of fact, the general administration of the government has, in the main, been admirable. Very little fault is to be found with the general details of the constitution or government, or with the manner of their administration; these have afforded large compensating advantages against the disorganizing tendencies of the democratic principles. The abrasions of the latter could not wear away in a day the conservative influences of the former.

Time is an important element in developing whatever of good or evil may reside in the social principles of a nation; and assuredly *less* time could not have been expected than has actually sufficed to bring out the vicious tendencies of the democratic polity, against all the counteracting influences that have been arrayed in opposition. Not the least of these influences is a conservative principle in human nature which protects society a great while against the worst social system that ever was devised. To say that society is composed of men is sufficient to account for the orderly working of any form of government for a considerable length of time. Man is essentially social in his nature; he bears within himself certain notions of order, of justice, of reason, with a strong desire to bring them into action, which compel him to live in the best organized society he can obtain. If his society be not the best, he will endure what he cannot cure; but he is much more inclined to cure than to endure. For this he labors unceasingly; and if his social system continue, his labor in the long run will not be in vain. Sooner or later he will make his social system fit his social nature, or conform to his social ideas, as the shell fits the oyster. For this *time* is needed; and also terrible violence is not unfrequently needed.

There is, therefore, in all societies, a wise reserve of popular good sense, which tends unceasingly to restrict political aberrations. The social spirit of this people possesses no inconsiderable degree of that conservative quality which capacitates them for resisting the disorganizing instincts of the worst social principles as long perhaps as any other people in the world. They have been not inaptly styled "Nature's democrats;" and the principle of self-government is, without doubt, the strongest of their social instincts. To arrange themselves into regularly organized bodies is as natural to them as breathing. This spirit of organization pursues them in all the relations of life. With no power stronger than their own *wills* to enforce obedience to the rules of their voluntary organizations, they are seldom found untrue to a due observance of them.

With such a people, then, for the base of a nation's population, and in view of that speculative inertia so common to large masses of persons, it is not wonderful that, up to this time, a certain amount of order should have been procured by this government, sufficient for the development of the national greatness, marvelous as it has been. Still less is our wonder excited when we reflect how short a time this security has lasted. The wonder is that it should have lasted no longer. No one looked to see it broken up so soon. And if this is to be considered the *terminus* of the national prosperity, or of the orderly working of the government, under the inspiration of the principles which have hitherto animated it, stronger proof could not be asked of the disorganizing tendency of those principles. And that this government, in its present form, has failed to answer the ends of its creation, and will progressively demonstrate its incapacity as time advances, shall be the business of this work to show.

But there is one other cause why this disorganization did not begin sooner; and this cause I shall do no more than designate, and pass on to other considerations. NUMBERS, also, as well as *time*, are needed to discover the vices of a political system like this. A sparse population, scattered over an almost endless extent of territory, would leave those vices undiscovered forever. Until very recently, the population of this country bore no proportion to its territory; nor does it do so even now, comparatively speaking. But up to the beginning of the present revolution, the rapidity of its increase had no parallel in history. If the same ratio of increase be renewed and continued, it will not be many generations before the land will be as overstocked with inhabitants as Belgium or China, or the most crowded nation in the world. When teeming millions are thrown together, and the dense masses are effervescing with the rank passions and ranker vices of human nature, then the effects, upon such multitudes, of the wild liberty of the democratic polity, must be left to the imagination to conceive.

Of course I can have no objection to self-government, nor to the largest liberty compatible with order. But license is not liberty; and the first principle of self-government is self-denial. It is the universal and absolute character claimed for the democratic dogmas, and their consequent excesses in practice, against which these strictures are directed. Of the right of liberty of conscience, and of the people to be represented in government, there is no manner of doubt. But these rights are relative, not absolute; they have their limitations and qualifications; and it is to define these that government is instituted. What else is meant by the word *government*, as well as by the thing itself, but the imposition of salutary restraints on unbounded liberty and the lawless exercise of natural rights? It is liberty with laws, and government without oppression, which society seeks.

The democratic polity, however, in effect not only ignores these restraints, but virtually seeks to restore man to what is supposed to have been his original state of nature, to the unqualified enjoyment of all natural rights, and to the wild liberty of untamed nature. That is, the tendency of those principles is that way; not that they would be able to land humanity in such a condition: the laws of human nature forbid it. This is not a forced construction of the tendency of the democratic doctrine. The design was actually avowed, in so many words, by a class of writers—I will not call them philosophers—of the French nation; for it is to France we must go to see this doctrine in its best aspect of consistency and power, not only in its practical workings at the most marked period of her Revolution, but in the pages of writers who best reflected the spirit of the age and people. The doctrine, as thus seen in France, at its highest point of culmination, represents civilization as an ever-growing degeneracy from the primitive ideal type; and that all political reformation must be regarded as destined to re-establish that primitive state. This original condition of man expresses the metaphysical notion, common to all modern metaphysicians, of a supposed state of nature, which is destined to become the invariable type of every social state. It is the metaphysical form of the old theological idea of the state of innocence and simplicity, in which man existed in Eden before the fall. Degraded from this happy mode of life by the commission of a crime known as *original sin*, he must now gradually work his way back by a series of political reforms. No social change can be considered a reform which does not tend to bring about this restoration. Democracy was thought to be an immense stride in that direction, since it seemed to release man from all political and moral restraints, and to elevate him at once to his original state of nature, and to the lost image of his Maker. This doctrine was not peculiar to Rousseau alone: that writer, by his urgent dialectics, only pushed it to its last consequences. It is the central idea of Schlegel's Philosophy of History, of his Philosophy of Life; and is reproduced in his Philosophy of Language. The French Revolution was, consciously or unconsciously, inaugurated to reduce it to practice. After displacing the old order, the French Revolution sought to re-establish in its stead a sort of metaphysical polytheism, something in the manner of the Greco-Roman system, as being nearer the primitive type. This, it will be seen at once, was nothing else but organizing, instead of a progression, a universal retrogradation; a substitution, for one decrepit system, of a more ancient and decrepit system still.*

The necessity for some sort of restraint on the wild liberty of the democratic polity, was of course felt by those eminent men who presided at the birth of this nation and assisted in organizing its government. An attempt was accordingly made to deprive the principle of the dangerous energy it had acquired while engaged in executing its revolutionary mission in Europe. This was believed to have been amply accomplished by the formation of a constitution so filled with checks and guards that it was thought a due balance was obtained which never could be destroyed. Results, however, have since demonstrated that the framers of the constitution were dealing with a principle more subtle than their sagacity; and that its wild liberty was not to be barred in one direction, while it was left free in another.

---

* See Comte's Positive Philosophy.

For example, the constitution recognized the existence of slavery; placed property in slaves on an equal footing with every other species of property; and made the most formal and solemn provision it could devise for its protection. At the same time, however, the dogmas of *popular sovereignty* and *equality* were recognized as co-ordinate principles of nature and society. According to these dogmas, "all men are born free and equal." Freedom and equality, therefore, are birthrights which all men inherit from nature, guaranteed to them by the laws of God, which laws society is bound to re-enact. Hence, the recognition of slavery by the constitution is treason against nature, against the laws of God, and against what ought to be laws of society. The constitution, therefore, is null and void *pro tanto;* and slavery, by a superior ordinance of nature, is an illegal institution. Thus was reached, as a last but necessary corollary of those dogmas, the "higher law" doctrine, which alone sufficed to release the democratic polity from the restraints put on it by the constitution.

From the same premises flows, by irresistible implication, the doctrine of *universal suffrage*, not less dangerous than the other, but infinitely more disgusting, as a practical measure of government. Universal suffrage is not a provision of the constitution; it is not specified as a necessary part of the republican form of government required by the constitution to be adopted by all the States; it is not obligatory on any State to adopt it as a clause of its constitution; it is an inference only, deduced, like the "higher law," from the democratic principles; and in order to carry those principles out as far as possible, according to their full intent and meaning, it came in time to be pretty generally adopted by most of the States.

When we look at the entire population—consisting of thirty millions as it now does in this country, or of sixty millions as it is likely soon to do—and consider the mass of ignorance, stupidity, vice, and corruption of which it is composed, nothing, surely, at first sight, could seem more revolting to common sense than an arrangement which would base government on such a mass of putrescence for a secure foundation. The "higher law" doctrine, viewed, for the first time, by the side of it, would appear reasonable and eminently proper. Nevertheless, we have not only seen the inference of universal suffrage admitted, but the right itself reduced to practice. It is now considered to be nothing more than an act of simple justice, due as well to one description of persons as to another. Indeed, the arrangement has long been regarded as the very best that could be devised by the wit of man, for the peace of society and the orderly working of government.

After witnessing the perpetration of an extravagance like that, and even becoming familiar with it and reconciled to it, and still remaining unconscious of any evils likely to flow from it,—after that, I say, we are not at liberty to sneer at the "higher law" doctrine, as an unauthorized derivative of the democratic principles, and as never likely to be adopted, as a political axiom, by any party. In effect, it has already been reduced to practice, and has borne its fruits. The passage of "Personal Liberty Laws" by certain States, in direct contravention of a law of Congress, on the ground that the latter was opposed to a law of God, is, to all intents and purposes, a practical application of that doctrine; and nothing but *time* is needed to translate it into a generally received maxim of government.

We have seen high public functionaries and individual States claiming, and even exercising, the right of construing the constitution according to their own understandings of it; and I have shown how irresistible is the deduction thence of the right of everybody else to do the same thing. Some of the ulterior consequences likely to flow from this practice have already been pointed out, and I shall not stop here to enumerate others. This pretended right is not less justly a derivative of the democratic principles than universal suffrage, or the higher law; nor is it more anarchical than they. The constitution and government would be just as apt to enjoy a perpetuity of existence under the patronage of one of these ideas as of another, or of all as of one. The right of individual interpretation of laws would have an equal chance, with both or either of the other two, of being, some time or other, transferred to practice, provided society, under existing circumstances, could last long enough to adopt it. The only difficulty in the way of democracy running itself out in practice to all its last consequences, is the want of time. Each sentiment is so disorganizing, that it dissolves society almost as soon as applied. If government had survived the inflictions of the democratic principles already adopted, there is no reason why *all* the extreme inferences authorized by the same polity should not, with equal propriety, follow, in regular order and in due course of time, those which preceded them. But the powers of social systems, like those of the human body, are limited, and intolerant of excesses. They will not endure to have too great a strain put on them. In the case of our government, the point of endurance would seem to have been passed; and we may now pronounce our social system to be in the articles of death.

On many accounts, the dogma of popular sovereignty is hostile to the perpetuity or long continuance of any constitution. The excellence of a constitution is no bar to the dissolving tendencies of such a principle. To what purpose make a constitution, and declare a sovereign power above it? How can a constitution be the supreme law of the land, and the people supreme also? All the explanations, which have ever been attempted, of this contradiction, have proved to be mere sophistries. Words can only conceal, they cannot reconcile, the contrariety. Facts are the best commentaries of the absurdity; and facts have demonstrated the impracticability of such a government. The sovereignty of the people is represented by the majority; and the majority rules. So long as the majority *choose* to respect the constitution, it is law; the submission of the majority is voluntary; there is no compulsory power to oblige obedience. Against the will of the majority, there are no guarantees for the continuance of the constitution from one day to another. Under such conditions, a constitution may govern, by courtesy, for seventy-five years, and fail on the seventy-sixth; or it may not last a single year, or even a day. In this country, there is a constant organization of the majority, capable of expressing its will at any moment. It is perfectly irresponsible, bound by no authority above itself, except an implied pledge of faith. Plighted faith might have some binding efficacy on an individual; but against the passions, the interests, the opinions, the moral sense of the multitude composing the majority, this bond is a mere rope of sand. The majority may interpret away the constitution, evade it, or put it away peremptorily. As the constitution exists only by the tolerance, so the rights of the minority exist only by the forbearance, of the majority: no sure guarantees are possible.

Under the auspices of the democratic dogmas, with their licentious inferences and latitudinous constructions, there is so much margin for evasions, that the majority need seldom resort to direct violations of the constitution in order to effect the worst purposes. The first method, which is the usual one, is even more intolerable than the other. There is some merit in a highway robber confronting you in the face of day and boldly demanding your purse; but none in a sneaking thief picking your pockets while persuading you of his honesty. In the first case, there are at least the virtues of courage and candor; in the other, nothing but fraud and cowardice. If I be robbed, what matters it to me whether there be a pretext or no pretext? whether there be a "higher law" or no law in heaven or on earth for it?

The "higher law" doctrine, flowing directly, as I have shown, from the democratic dogmas, leads to the rejection of all municipal laws which may happen to be offensive to the *moral sense* of a community: the passage thence to its *interests* is an easy one. Under such a law, the abolition or the confiscation of property, so far from being difficult, is almost inevitable. On pretense of conscientious scruples, this doctrine led *vir-*

tually to the repudiation of the constitution on the subject of slavery, and to the nullification of laws passed by Congress for the more effectual execution of the constitutional provisions on that subject. In effect, this is nothing more nor less than the abrogation of laws made for the protection of property. The *species* of property, thus taken away from the guardianship of the law, makes no difference in the case. If the majority assume the right of annulling the law in the respect of one description of property, it will find, or create, a pretext for withdrawing some other kind from legal protection.

Here is revealed the most dangerous, the most revolutionary and anarchical tendency yet betrayed by the fundamental dogmas of our government. It clearly indicates the necessary proclivity of the democratic instincts toward that social vortex, the abolition or confiscation of *all* property, which, whenever it is reached, will engulf society in irretrievable ruin. Nor is this the first manifestation of the tendency of popular sovereignty in that fatal direction. We are not left in doubt as to its capacity that way. Its genius for such work has been too often displayed, for us ever again to mistake its power or inclination to repeat the same rôle whenever the opportunity offers. History is not silent on this part of its performances. In Rome, more than two thousand years ago, when popular sovereignty was in the ascendency, it established a precedent on that subject, which has ever since been quoted, as high authority, by the *tribunes* of the people everywhere. The Agrarian law of the Roman plebeians has been held up, for imitation, to all subsequent ages which have witnessed the temporary domination of the populace. The division of property made in Rome, under that law, took place under political circumstances but little, if at all, different from the social conditions which have obtained in this country; and the tendency of things here, so far, points to a similar catastrophe.

Or, if we need an example of more modern date, it is to France again we must go in order to obtain a presentment of what popular sovereignty is capable of doing in this as in other respects. Whether it be in ancient or in modern times, in Rome or in France, mankind is ever the same; and, under similar circumstances, will always act in pretty much the same way. *Cœlum, non animum, mutant, qui trans mare currunt;* the mere crossing the Atlantic alters not the human mind: popular sovereignty, under whatever sky it plays its fantastic tricks, will still repeat itself; its *animus* is the same in America as in Rome, as in France; and, until the organization of humanity be changed, its conduct will vary but little anywhere.

In France, then, the organs of democracy, at the epoch of its highest intensification, announced in so many words that "all property is robbery;" and though no *agrarian law* was ever passed, that measure was warmly advocated, and at one time became, next to the guillotine, the most threatening aspect of the Revolution. The preoccupation of the actors in the more stirring scenes of their bloody drama suspended, for the moment, this crowning Act of the Piece; and the reaction, which in happy hour set in, snatched that distracted country from the very jaws of *agrarianism.* Nothing but a little more *time* was needed for popular sovereignty to run, on that occasion, the full circuit of its usual career. Under the whip and spur, which put it to such high speed in the French Revolution, it broke down before it could complete the last "quarter stretch" to the goal which is the inevitable *terminus* of its natural life. It met a premature ruin in the excess of its velocity; and in its untimely end consisted the safety of society.

Nevertheless, during the short period of its rapid existence, it found time to confiscate nearly half the property of the nation, and not only to impoverish, but to expatriate the wealthiest citizens of the land, for no other crime but their obtrusive opulence. The possession of such large estates, beyond the necessary wants of the owners, was in the highest degree offensive to the *moral sense* of this conscientious principle. The proprietors of those estates were, in many instances, guillotined for the unpardonable sin of inheriting patrimonies which "robbed" of the necessaries of life so many persons better than they, or as good. For these involuntary crimes against the *moral sense* or the *interests* of popular sovereignty, the representatives of the nation's wealth and power were inexorably decimated. The proscription began at the top of society; and the king himself was beheaded for the unintentional offense of having been unconsciously born to the inheritance of a crown. As the heirships of fortunes and high social positions entailed upon the hapless possessors the hereditaments of crime and punishment, the decapitations and confiscations were rapidly descending to the lowest culprits, when the recoil rescued the country from the oppression of its multitudinous tyrants, and consigned it to the tender mercies of a solitary despot.

It must not be forgotten that these deeds were enacted in the bosom of the foremost nation of the world, at the most enlightened period of its history; that the ranks of popular sovereignty, on that memorable occasion, contained some of the first men of the nation, or of the age, or of any age or nation; that the *alumni* of learning, of science, of art, of eloquence, statesmanship, and war—sages, heroes, patriots, philanthropists—all that were esteemed wise and good—flocked with the rest to this standard of democracy, as symbolizing the cause of civilization itself; that they identified the highest social interests of humanity with the democratic principles, which were believed to be the renovators of society, and destined to carry it forward to perfection. We must not, therefore, repeat the common error of supposing it was the rabble only who enlisted in this frightful crusade. The rabble were there undoubtedly, all of them, in full force, a terrible array! the very orgie of Sans-Culottism! It was mainly into their hands the Revolution ultimately fell; and it was they, principally, who carried it out of the benevolent designs in which it originated. They and their deeds were the *ultimatum* of the Revolution, its last but necessary corollaries, its real conclusions. The democratic principles, the premises from which those extreme consequences were drawn, were not wholly innocent of the horrid deductions; they authorized all the excesses which were perpetrated in their name. In spite of those extravagances, and the signal failure of the democratic principles to accomplish any of the marvels expected of them, some of the first men of France, and elsewhere, remained firm in the democratic faith to the last. The

Gracchi were the best and noblest of the Romans, they were the "jewels of the State," brave, generous, humane; and yet their zeal for the popular cause hurried them beyond the bounds of moderation and justice. They passed the agrarian law from the purest of motives; and their lives fell a sacrifice to the energy of their honesty.

SOCIALISM, a new term for *agrarianism*, and almost the synonym of *popular sovereignty*, is so essentially an offshoot of the democratic principles, that we can scarcely doubt the *rôle* it is destined to play here some day or other. This phrase is identical with *communism*, a new French word corresponding with *radicalism*. The idea it covers came into France cotemporaneously with the democratic principles, or rather was suggested by them at a very early period of their advent. Like other democratic dogmas, it has ever since struggled for life in European societies; but it is there kept down by the strong hand of heavily armed governments.

Many years ago, *socialism* crossed the Atlantic, and attempted to naturalize itself in this country. But it was soon put to rest here by the cheap lands, the abundant resources, and the wondrous facilities for making not only livelihoods, but fortunes. Its arrival hither was premature. None of the conditions of the times or country were favorable to its immediate success. It accordingly retired from the busy surface of society. But it sleeps only: it is not dead; and may at any moment start into active life and gigantic proportions.

Hitherto, *confiscation* was with us an idea only. It was something about which we had heard and read a great deal; but the practice of it was associated in our minds with times of violence and with nations but imperfectly civilized. It was thought to be a relic of barbarism not at all applicable to our society. The progress of civilization, the organization of justice on higher and better understood principles, the enlightenment of education, and the superior claims of a mild and beneficent Christianity were deemed to have left that method of spoliation far behind in past ages when men were cruel and rapacious. Confiscation has ever been a convenient and fruitful pretext for the gratification of the black passions of revenge and cupidity. It is at best but a species of legalized robbery. Avarice and hatred alone conspired to keep it alive during the worst periods of history. We have shuddered as we perused those records of barbarity; and have congratulated ourselves on being elevated, by the terms of our civilization, far above the reach of cruelties the practice of which degraded men to the level of savages. While we have witnessed, in the pages of history, human beings preying upon each other like wild beasts, stripping each other of rights, of property, of everything calculated to make life endurable, we have blessed the religion, the laws, the education which rescued us from the possibility of such a fate. Confiscation is unknown to our constitution. It has never found a place in our statutes. It is passing away from modern usages everywhere; and is fast becoming an anacronism of the age. The most advanced nations practice it sparingly, or not at all.

But all this is now changed. Confiscation has ceased to be with us a mere idea. Its practice is no longer a novelty. It is not now, as formerly, one of the hearsays of history, terrifying us with the bare recital of its cruelties. We have already familiarized our minds with its performances. We have invoked it from the musty traditions of the past. The law of nations, enacted ages before our society was born, has furnished us with precedents for its use. The change has been like a turn of the kaleidoscope. In a single day our civilization has receded many centuries. Barbarities, thought to be obsolete, are revived; and we are not so much shocked by their presence, as we were wont to be by their narratives. We travel in a circle. We are playing the same history over again. Our social ideas are turning back into old political grooves; and we are seeking, in the exploded institutions of rude epochs, for models which, in our estimation, are alone worthy of imitation.

This war was begun with confiscations on a large scale by both parties. Each party aimed to fill its empty treasury by despoiling innocent individuals of their private property. The millions to be thus appropriated were coolly calculated. There seem to have been no compunctious visitings of conscience for this act of treachery, which was as cruel to the unsuspecting victims as it was unworthy a great people. Never was there a punishment more undeserved. The crime for which these persons suffered was that of residing in one section of the country and owning property in the other. They had all their lives been in the habit of considering both sections as their common country. They could not serve both sides—and perhaps were unwilling to serve either side against the other. Their affections and their interests were equally divided. They gloried in the grandeur of the united nation, and would have laid down their lives for its preservation against foreign aggression. Since the foundation of the government, the laws and customs of either section had invited the capital and labor of the other, with not only an implied but an expressed pledge of protection. The intercourse was mutual and unreserved. Their capital and labor had enriched both sections. No suspicion of treachery was entertained. In an hour they were betrayed. No sufficient time was allowed them to secure the fruits of their honest toil. Without any fault of theirs, they were mercilessly delivered over to plunder, under the imposing name of confiscation. This, then, was the impotent conclusion of the boasted progress of the age. It was to obtain such results that man has suffered so much and so long. He has drenched the world with his blood to secure immunity against oppression and injustice; and in the end he finds himself suddenly turned back to the age of Grotius, and Puffendorf, and Vattel. Democracy, "the last hope of humanity," has been able to conduct society only to this bad eminence, and a reproduction of antiquated barbarisms is the sum of its vaunted reforms. This is treading back its footsteps to its favorite "state of nature" with frightful speed.

It is useless to attempt to fasten the blame of all this upon any section. The administration at Washington, acting as the organ of abolitionism, threatens to confiscate the property of eight millions of citizens, amounting to countless billions of dollars' worth, just as soon as it can obtain the power to do so. This threat was not prompted wholly by a sense of justice. The rebellion will be but the *pretext* for the anarchical principle now presiding at the seat of government, to gratify one of its strongest instincts. The execution of the threat, if carried out to the full extent promised, will be more monstrous even than secession itself. Thousands of persons will fall victims to it who were as innocent of secession as babes unborn. Secession may be suppressed, and good may be extracted from it; but the other will be an unmitigated evil, the fatal consequences of which will pursue the nation to its grave. Confiscation is neither just nor generous. Good citizens were never made by such means. It neither deters from guilt nor superinduces penitence. It is a punishment fit for slaves, not for freemen. It is unworthy the dignity and true manhood of human nature, and indicates no progress made in the science of government or in enlightened culture. If Christianity and universal education—the peculiar boast of the age—can-prompt to no loftier deeds, then they, too, must be counted among the mournful failures of human experiments. Like the constitution and government of this country,—both so admirable in themselves,—Christianity, the daughter of Heaven, and Education, her handmaiden, are neutralized by the pernicious influences of social principles which dissipate the human mind in endless abstractions, and in futile efforts to realize ideas which are hostile to both order and progress. As we advance further in this investigation, we shall be more and more convinced of the truth of this assertion. Each step we take will not only strengthen our conviction, but will aid in conducting us to a solution of the present difficulties of our situation. We have seen some of the effects of popular sovereignty. There is another product of this dogma, which imparts to it peculiar vitality and efficacy, which must now be noticed, and its place assigned in this general disorganizing and demoralizing process. That product is the

DEMAGOGUES.

The effervescence incident to the working of such a composition as our social system threw in time to the surface of society, as it was bound to do, a class of persons of all others the most dangerous in a government like this. Without the demagogues, the masses would be innocent and democracy harmless. But the demagogues, thus developed, are the natural consequence and complement of the system. The dogma of popular sovereignty, with its universal suffrage and majority rule, having introduced the populace on the stage of politics, and made them the dictators of society, they must of course, in order to discharge their functions, supply themselves with organs. These organs must represent, as near as possible, their own intellectual caliber, express their ideas, cater to their passions, and subserve their interests. The kind of persons thus to be acted on, the means to be employed, and the ends to be obtained must tend to remove elevated minds and superior understandings from a political career, and to deliver over the government to charlatanism and inferiority. Accordingly, presumptuous and enterprising mediocrity has never before had so fortunate a chance. Popular sovereignty has covered over the whole surface of society with these social parasites, and consigned the government almost exclusively to their hands. Of course they can do no otherwise than work out their own political ideas, and bring down the administration of government to the level of their own moral and intellectual training. As that standard falls far below the ideal of a pure Christianity and an ever-advancing civilization, which tends to social perfection, it must contradict their aspirations, and remain an obstacle to progress, until eliminated by *revolution*, or by a rational method of reform.

The demagogues are a sort of summary or resumé of all the vices of our political system. They represent it, in its least favorable aspect, more correctly than any other single feature can pretend to do. A detailed and accurate description of the demagogues, would give a very clear and precise notion of the system generally. Belonging to a low social *status*,—commonly without much education, without mental discipline, without virtue or common honesty, without fortune; negative in all things but an ill-concealed hatred, not of wealth, but of the wealthy, not of respectability, but of the respectable,—the demagogues yet possess a wondrous mental activity, more of the character of cunning than intelligence. This cunning compensates, in some degree, their ignorance, since it serves their bad ends more effectually than the best education or the most cultivated intelligence could do without it. The restless activity of their minds, thus guided by shrewdness, and untrammeled by the restraints of an enlightened conscience, is more than a match for the intellectual inertia of the masses, on whom they operate. With little interest in the welfare of the country, and regardless of consequences, they will, to serve their selfish ends, cater to the worst passions of the multitude, on whom they depend for their elevation. They are to the multitude what the vital principle is to the body. They are the head, the brain, of which the people are the working members. They make the people acquainted with their own passions, their wants, their desires. They tell them their rights, their power, their influence in the government. Abundantly supplied with political clap-traps, and with a rude eloquence compounded of Billingsgate and anecdotes, they can and do, when the occasion comes about, inflame to a white-heat the passions of the multitude, which are then manifested like the torrent and the whirlwind. In return, the people surrender themselves to their guidance, make them the exclusive managers of public affairs, and elevate them, upon their shields, as it were, like the old Roman soldiers, to the head of the government. And for this elevation they claim, like the Pretorian guards, the usual bounty bestowed on such occasions.

Here, then, is a combination which embodies the most stupendous political power that can be conceived of, and which no government or nation on earth can long withstand. It is a combination which mobilizes the masses, and gives to democracy all its capacity for evil; for the government thus administered is bound to reflect the passions of the multitude, and to reproduce their ideas. Without this alliance, the demagogues would be powerless, the masses motionless, democracy harmless, and—shall I say it?—this war had never been begun, nor this work written.

EQUALITY.

This dogma, one of the three elements of the democratic trinity, has only been considered incidentally, in connection with the other two, as constituting a unity. If it be separated, and treated by itself, it will be found not less disorganizing than the others. Like liberty of conscience, or free inquiry, it is taken to be absolute when it is only relative, and permanent while it expresses merely the attitude of minds engaged in breaking up the old system. When the dogma of equality, in connection with its associate principles, had achieved the overthrow of the theological and military *regime*, it could not become otherwise than destructive to any new organization of society that might be attempted upon its suggestion, because its activity must then be directed against the basis of any new classification whatever; for, of course, any division of society into classes must be inconsistent with the equality claimed for all.*

It has been justly said, that many truths lose their force by repetition. The most absurd fallacies are perpetuated by similar means. They are repeated until they are believed in. Being handed down to us as traditional truths, they are accepted, without examination, as mere matters of course. The mind, from early familiarity with them, never thinks of questioning their claims to veracity. This is especially true of many of the social maxims of modern times. For eighty-seven years we

* See Comte's admirable remarks on this subject, in his Positive Philosophy.

have repeated so often the *ad captandum* assertion that "all men are created equal," until we have at last brought ourselves to accept it as an ascertained fact. No amount of experience and observation, nor the most contradictory reasons, seem capable of shaking this belief from its fast anchorage in the modern mind. It is an error so transparent that we have but to open our eyes to see it, and yet we have repeated it into a truism which it is treason against common sense to question. "The inalienable rights of man" are spoken of with as undoubting faith as if they really existed; and "right reason," the most undefined of all verbal imposture, is appealed to, as the conclusive foundation of this puerile card-house of rickety abstractions. If these crotchets had confined themselves to Fourth-of-July orations, there would have been little need to interrupt a pleasant delusion; but when serious attempts are made to apply them practically, and to form out of them a system of government upon which depends the welfare of society and the happiness of humanity, then, like other time-honored fallacies, they must be weighed in the balances.

The period of the American Revolution, when Mr. Jefferson, acting as the organ of the American Congress, brought forth his celebrated "Declaration of Independence," was the epoch of greatest political disturbance in the world. The cause of this disturbance has already been stated. Few minds, even of the largest caliber, can resist being influenced by the popular sentiments of the age in which they live. Mr. Jefferson very truly reflected the spirit of his; and was so adapted to the disposition of his cotemporaries, that he became, with remarkable success, the most veritable organ of the revolutionary movement of the times. The Declaration of Independence, which he has the credit of composing, contains a pretty accurate summary of some of the most conspicuous revolutionary sentiments of the age, which, in this country, were christened with the name of *democratic principles*. Among them, the dogma of *equality* is rendered very prominent, and is made universal and absolute by an unqualified assertion of it.

Thus considered, the principle of equality abrogates the most conspicuous arrangement anywhere to be seen in the universe, and reduces all things to that dead level said to be hateful to gods and men. Certainly nothing can be more abhorrent to nature than the equality here asserted, for nowhere in her domain do we see anything at all resembling it. If in the external world we see no manifestation of any such principle, much less is it visible in the moral world. It is not possible to make men equal, because they are not so. Nature has stamped them with an ineradicable inequality which no artifice can displace. Nor are they equivalent: the differences are not compensatory; they are unqualified, and mark an ascending and descending scale, the extremities of which are as far asunder as the poles. In no state of association, therefore, can men possess an identity of rights, beyond that of equal protection by the laws; and the society which does not meet these natural disparates by some corresponding social arrangement, is only preparing trouble for itself; the friction and irritation caused by this want of fitness will allow humanity no rest until it make its social state fit all the natural inequalities which exist in itself. Of all the disparates, of which the world is so full, none are so marked as moral and intellectual inequalities. And while these superior diversities, already so conspicuous in a natural way, are being continually increased by the progress of civilization, the simpler kinds, which most attract the attention of superficial observers, are diminished in the same proportion.

Since the advent of the democratic polity, an unusual amount of attention has been given to the education of the people, with the hope, no doubt, of elevating them, by that means, to the level of their pretensions. Too much cannot be said in favor of education; it deserves all the encomiums which have been heaped upon it. But what education can do for the people is very little indeed, compared with the grand results, and the kind of results, expected of it. It can supply no faculty which nature has denied, nor enlarge any which she has dwarfed. It cannot make Newtons out of numskulls, nor Clays out of clowns: with all the education in the world, the dunce will still plod on in his native dullness; and without it, genius, like the skylark, will still waft its notes to heaven from the furrow in the field. So questionable is the benefit which education (so called) confers upon those minds to whom nature has been least bountiful, that in many cases a deterioration rather than an improvement characterizes the result. Nature would thus seem to resent man's futile efforts to disarrange her plans; for, so far from allowing her discrepancies to be diminished, and all men and things to be blurred into one undistinguishable mass, the very artifices used for that purpose are made, by her contrivance, to increase her disparates, and to magnify the varieties in which she delights. For while, in a well-regulated society, inferior minds receive very little advantage from education, and are sometimes damaged by it, the amount of development of which the highest orders of faculties are susceptible, and which they derive from education, is almost incalculable. Were there none but common men in it, the world would wait long for a statue of Appelles, a play of Shakspeare, a composition of Mozart, and then not get them, though it were full to repletion of what is commonly called education. Homer composed his grand epic with perhaps little or no knowledge of the art of reading and writing. Some of the greatest men that ever lived scarcely ever saw the inside of a school-house. Of the thousands annually sent forth from the walls of modern universities, rarely does one confer honor on himself or his country. The scientific marvels, which are transforming the world, are the products of comparatively few great men, most of whom get their education pretty much as the bird gets its song. Without these rare souls, who cannot be prevented from learning, Europe and America would be at this day what Africa is, and ever has been, and ever will be, with no other but the negro race to transform it.

To apply, then, the doctrine of equality to any assemblage of persons thus widely constituted and differently developed, is to ignore the most obvious arrangement of nature, and to violate the simplest law of natural justice. Disparities thus fixed by nature are ineradicable, and it is the first duty of society to provide for them; otherwise the dogma of equality, which seeks to obliterate them, becomes anarchical, and directly hostile to its original destination. It remains, moreover, an obstacle to progress; no amelioration of any society, whose deliberations it sways, can be hoped for while its influence lasts. If it be not otherwise extruded from the mind of society, then its elimination by revolution is inevitable; for no society can long exist in the state of anarchy which its disorganizing tendencies superinduce. As we have seen, however, the absolute equality of the whole human race, from their very birth, is dogmatically asserted in Mr. Jefferson's Declaration of Independence; and this doctrine of perfect equality, without the slightest qualification, has ever since retained its original importance in the politics of this nation. The raid which John Brown made into Virginia not many years ago was mainly inspired by this fanatical sentiment. That hostile incursion into a peaceable State, at a period of profound national tranquillity, was called by John Brown and his partisans a "continuation of the war of liberty and *equality* which was begun in '76," and was justified by the equality clause in Mr. Jefferson's Declaration of Independence. It was the prelude to the present revolution, in which the doctrine of equality is deeply implicated.

During the fervor of the French Revolution—for it is still to that epoch of French history we must go (I hope it shall be our last visit) to see the working also of this democratic principle when run out to its last consequences—the dogma of equality played so important a part in that terrible drama that, for nearly ten years, the *Sans-Culottes* were the virtual masters of the nation. When the revolution broke out, the leveling process was the first begun, and the last discontinued. The *Sans-Culottic status* was the prescribed social, moral, and intellectual standard for the entire population. None were allowed to ascend above it, and none could descend below it. Aristocracy was the highest crime known to the *Sans-Culottic* code: not only the offense was in all cases capital, but the bare suspicion of it was punished with instant death and confiscation. Even the scientific spirit was stigmatized as tending to institute an aristocracy of knowledge, which was as offensive as any other species of aristocracy. Many innocent persons accordingly had their heads chopped off for no other reason than because they were suspected of containing a little too much learning. Genius, talents, respectability, or moral worth of any kind above the prescribed standard, was a sure passport to the inevitable *guillotine*. So obnoxious was wealth, or fine clothes, or any other distinguishing mark of superiority, that the opulent and fashionable, to save their lives, affected poverty and the *blouse*, and the red flannel night-cap was seen on every head. I have already noticed the narrow escape of the French nation, at that epoch, from the horrors of *agrarianism;* and it was mainly to the dogma of *equality* that the peril was due.

It is useless to say that all the examples I have quoted from the French Revolution were portentous or eccentric incidents; that they were extreme consequences, or exceptional cases; that they occurred at a period of national disorganization or national insanity; that that sort of thing is now played out, and can never happen again. Their legitimate descent from the democratic principles is evident and certain. They were logical corollaries of the premises whence they flowed. They were the natural effects of those doctrines when considered as absolute and released from governmental restraints. If they occurred at a period of national disorganization or insanity, it was they that disorganized the nation, or deprived it of its reason. Similar causes produce similar effects: as soon as all the conditions favorable to a luxuriant development of the democratic polity are fulfilled in this country, that polity cannot fail to re-enact similar scenes here.

The present war affords ample proof of this assertion. The events transpiring around me at this moment differ but little from the worst scenes of the French Revolution. None but they who are spectators of them, and have oracular proof of their reality, could believe in their existence in the last half of the nineteenth century, and in a Christian nation. Before their actual occurrence they would have seemed to us impossible. They now indicate that civilization has made but little permanent progress in this country. They show how easy is a relapse toward barbarism when society is not secured by the salutary restraints of government, and when fanatical sentiments can take it out of the rules of order and consign it to such disorderly courses. It is not in times of peace, when men's passions are at rest, that we can judge of the soundness of a nation's constitution: it is periods of disturbance which test the efficacy of its social principles. When the fanaticism of any number of persons, however considerable, can upset government, and in the name of law and under the sanction of legal authority perpetrate the most horrid outrages against justice and humanity, it is evident that that government was never settled upon a solid basis, and that its political principles have mortally corrupted the minds of its subjects. Modern civilization, among the most advanced nations of Europe, has marked its progress, not only by ameliorating the forms of civil government and diminishing the *causes* of active hostilities, but also, in an especial manner, by softening the ruder features of war when hostilities do occur. Under these benign reforms, war never inflicts its cruelties on private citizens. The property and persons of non-belligerents and the general harmony of society are as much respected by an invading army as if it were a time of peace.

The war now raging in this country has gone back several centuries for the method of its conduct; and the remark is equally applicable to both sides. The passions of hatred and revenge seem to animate the two governments in a large degree, and to descend with increasing bitterness through the officers to the common soldiers. These savage and ferocious sentiments are participated in by large majorities of the people of both sections. On the part of one of the belligerents, the war has been used as a pretext for confiscating a larger amount of private property than was ever before known in the history of the world; and a more reckless disregard of the commonest rights of humanity and of the higher claims of civilization was never exhibited even in the days of remotest barbarism. In the last analysis, these base passions and cruel practices are clearly referable to the demoralizing tendencies of our social principles. The fanaticism inspired by those principles, and not the exigencies of the war, as pretended, was the real cause of the Emancipation Proclamation, which has robbed non-belligerents of such an enormous amount of private property. The war, too, has called forth many ostentatious exhibitions of the hatred which has rankled so long in the bosoms of the fanatics of the North against what they supposed to be the aristocratical sentiments engendered by slavery in the Southern mind. Their animosity seems to have been excited principally by envy, and by a hatred, not of slavery, but of slave-owners. The possession of so many slaves was fatal to that equality which it was the duty of this government to establish. I have seen in Northern newspapers letters, purporting to come from the Federal army, declaring that the war must not end until these aristocratical pretensions were "*thrashed*" out of the Southern mind, and that domineering people were brought by poverty and oppression to a proper sense of their insignificance.

If we pursue the dogma of equality to its practical consequences in this society, we shall discover that it is the same monster here it was in the French Revolution; and that its offspring in both countries bear a family-likeness too striking to be mistaken. We all know the prejudice existing here against *aristocracy*. Though the law make it not a punishable offense, it is little less than a crime in the estimation of popular opinion; and the bare imputation of being an *aristocrat* is enough to consign the suspected individual to obloquy and ridicule, if not to positive hatred and detestation. In spite of this prejudice, in no country in the world is the *sentiment* of aristocracy stronger than here; but as yet it is cherished in secret, and publicly denied. Already it animates private circles, and it is beginning slily to influence social relations in many ways too visible to be overlooked. It thus manifests itself in society, because it exists in human nature, and is equally irrepressible in both. If it be not recognized *formally* and regulated by legal enactments, it will get itself recognized *informally* and regulated by methods so awkward as to breed secret hatreds and ultimately open hostilities.

Liberty of conscience, from which is derived the dogma of equality, implies the most fundamental of all equalities—the equality of intelligence. But it is precisely in the moral and intellectual sphere that the greatest and most radical of all inequalities is found to exist. It is the difference between virtue and vice, between genius and stupidity. The highest specimens of humanity fall but "little below the angels," the lowest rise but little above the brutes. There is a moral and social, as well as a physical law of gravity. The most virtuous and intelligent minds naturally gravitate toward the highest places in society; and to these places, for the good of all and the benefit of society, they are justly entitled. It is preposterous to suppose that large masses of depraved men could ever live a great while together without the stringent bonds of successive gradations, having the main governing strength in the apex. This is so obviously one of the natural checks that ought to be incorporated into every social system, that it is surprising how it could be deliberately excluded from the constitution of any government. The exclusion cannot fail to produce social irregularities, particularly where the opposite or democratic element is retained by itself and reigns alone. Nevertheless, to this exclusion, permanently and systematically, all the democratic dogmas are irrevocably compromited.

Habit is said to be *second nature*. *A habit of thinking* has so much of *first nature* in it, that it is a perfectly safe foundation for any system we may choose to build upon it. The *habit of thinking* that "some are born to command and others to obey," established most of the despotisms of antiquity. Upon the *habit of thinking* that "the powers that be are ordained of God," was founded the practice of "passive obedience and non-resistance;" it also supported the law of "legitimacy," by which a certain person, whether he were virtuous or vicious, a wise man or a fool, had, by reason of his birth alone, and to the utter exclusion of everybody else, the undoubted right to govern, and, at his sovereign will and pleasure, to take away the lives of his subjects, and to do without question or restraint any and every thing else he might have a mind to. The *habit of thinking* that the first-born son had the right to inherit all the family honors and property, established the law of *primogeniture*, and not only reconciled younger brothers and sisters to the arrangement, but made them rejoice at and glory in the provisions of a law which, while it consigned them to poverty and obscurity, transmitted the estate entire to their elder brother. This *habit of thinking* has so far displaced what we would call *first nature*, that fathers and mothers have eagerly consigned their daughters to the gloomy prison of a convent, and their younger sons to the church or army, to insure their celibacy, that no remnant of the family might remain, but the heir, to impair the future integrity of the estate. If we go further back to more remote times and nations —to ancient India, for instance—we shall find institutions still more monstrous (to our mode of thinking) similarly supported. In short, there is no enormity in government or morals which, to a deep-rooted and inveterate *habit of thinking*, may not seem perfectly natural and eminently right and proper.

When a reaction, whether of a moral or a material force, sets in, it seldom stops at that *juste milieu*, that half-way ground, where alone safety resides. If, in a moral sense, it start from one extreme point of absurdity, it is almost certain to rush to the opposite extremity which is not less absurd. Such has been precisely the effect upon the human mind of its emancipation, by the doctrine of liberty of conscience and its derivative dogmas, from those antiquated *habits of thought*, which detained it so long, and perpetrated, in the name of "right reason," absurdities which, to our *habits of thinking*, seem too monstrous for belief. The reaction, however, as in most cases it is so apt to do, has hurried forward the human mind into other excesses, different indeed in kind, but not at all less in degree. A deep-rooted and inveterate *habit of thinking* that "all men are created equal," and that it is impossible to make them otherwise, that the people are the legitimate sovereigns, the only true fountain of all power, and that they and they alone are entitled to govern, is now gradually establishing another state of things not less monstrous and absurd than that which has been abandoned. Entertaining, then, an undisturbed belief in their own supremacy and infallibility, in the indefeasible equality and liberty of all men, and in the duty of society to organize these principles and carry them out to their full intent and meaning, the people cannot do else than look with extreme loathing and disgust upon pretensions of a contrary tendency. All assumptions of superiority from any other quarter, and whatever tends to limit their authority, are met with suspicions and jealousies. They are taught that there is nothing more difficult in the management of the affairs of a nation than of a family: that it is the juggle of keeping up impositions to blind the eyes of the vulgar, that constitutes the intricacy of state: that the mysticism of inequality has been the sole cause of all the evils attendant upon human nature: that any man in society may fill any place in government, and exercise its functions. Under the influence of these tuitions, and having all the political power in their hands by the convenient methods of universal suffrage and the ballot-box, they admit to public offices none but persons of their own caste and their flatterers. Vagabonds and loafers, men utterly incapable of managing their own affairs, are not unfrequently intrusted with the mismanagement of the affairs of the nation. The demagogues are at the same time the creatures and the masters of the people. The demagogues control the government by feeding the passions and prejudices of the multitude, and by gratifying their desires. By reason of their representative character, of their approximation to the level of the masses, of their low moral and intellectual caliber, the demagogues exclude the best men of the nation from the service of the state by usurping those places which ae-justly due to the latter.

This state of things cannot last. The momentum which brought society to this condition is necessarily progressive. It cannot remain stationary. It must obey the original impetus which set it in motion, and continue, with an ever-increasing velocity, to proceed from bad to worse, until it meets its ruin in its own extremity. In spite, then, of these complacent notions of popular power and equality, the movement of society is perpetually widening the breach between the *ideas* of the people and the *reality* of things, between their social *theories* and their social *conditions*. Population increases faster than wealth, and the tendency of wealth is to concentrate itself into the fewest number of hands. The numerical increase of the poor, therefore, as compared with the rich, is in the compound ratio of those two tendencies; and the interval between poverty and wealth, between the poor and the rich, is perpetually widening in the same proportion: the rich are ever growing richer, and the poor poorer; the former are ever becoming proportionally fewer, and the latter more numerous.

Very soon, therefore, the people will begin to see palaces rising around them, while they live in huts. They will see men, apparently without labor, surfeited with the luxuries of wealth, while they eat the hard bread of poverty, earned by the sweat of their brows. These, and many other contrasts not less violent, while they contradict the people's preconceived notions of universal equality and popular sovereignty, cannot fail to rouse their indignation, and to direct their hostility against what to them will seem an abnormal condition of society too intolerable to be borne. All this time their faith in their social theories will in no degree have diminished; they will rather have gained strength every day. Their efforts, therefore, will be unceasing to conform their social state to their social ideas. They will know but too well, by *habits of thought* contracted from infancy, by the lessons of experience acquired at the ballot-box, by the teachings of the demagogues at the hustings, by their daily conversations among themselves, by the promptings of vanity and conceit never extinct in even the lowest natures, that they have the right and the *power*, *legally* or by *revolution*, to reform in society whatever they may consider to be abuses. The pangs of present sufferings, the forebodings of future misery, the growing inequalities of classes will not be likely to diminish their violence, or to moderate their innovations. The constitution will be no bar to their reformatory action. They have long ago learnt to construe that instrument according to their own ideas; and all laws which contradict the fundamental principles of absolute equality and popular sovereignty, or any other natural right, are, by their interpretations of them, *ipso facto* nugatory and of non-effect. Practice must and shall be made to agree with precept. They will have already seen their favorite dogmas wage successfully one stupendous war, and, under the flimsy pretext of "military necessity," maintain their supremacy by confiscating an incalculable amount of private property, and by reducing to their own pecuniary level eight millions of opulent proprietors. The habits engendered by that war, confirming their habits of thought, will have familiarized them with deeds of spoliation. The burning, destroying, appropriating the superfluities of wealth will no longer be the "scarecrows" of their imaginations. Tradition, the fireside tales of those performances, enhanced by distance and the embellishments of fancy, will make it comparatively easy to reproduce them in some other form, and on a scale not less grand. Whenever, therefore, a war of castes shall break out in densely populated communities here, as sooner or later it is bound to do with such a political system as ours, the horrors of the French Revolution will at last find a parallel in the enormities of this.

The disturbances which took place in Northern communities, soon after the declaration of war by Mr. Lincoln, and subsequently the riots in New York, had, it is true, nothing of this character in them; they were not occasioned by any hostility to aristocracy. But they bear witness to the dangerous social element that is gradually maturing in those populous communities; to the intolerant spirit of the rabble when their ideas or passions are opposed; and to the merciless character of their vengeance when roused.

To this it may be replied, that such perturbations as those referred to are not peculiar to this society: that they are of as rare occurrence here as elsewhere: that they have happened to other communities as well; and are liable to break out in any nation. My answer is, *not necessarily.* They never occur except in nations that are dominated by a libertine soldiery or a no less libertine democracy. They took place in Rome at epochs when the plebeians, and subsequently the Pretorian guards, had the ascendency there; in Turkey, under the domination of the Janizaries; in France, of the *Sans-Culottes;* and in other nations, upon the sudden irruption of democracy, before it could be suppressed. But, in this nation, they are a *necessary* element of its social system; and are bound, sooner or later, to break forth when occasion or opportunity offers. They are inevitable to the natural working of the fundamental principles of our society; and though they may be detained long in inactivity, a *time* will come, with increase of population and the growing disparity between wealth and numbers, when they will manifest themselves like the tornado and the earthquake.

Already, in the most crowded sections, where society, fermented by principles so disorganizing, has thrown off an undue proportion of demagogues, social agitations have been attempted of the most pernicious description, and so far suppressed only by the indifference of popular good sense, by the ridicule of the intelligent or conservative classes, and by the difficulty of putting in motion the lower orders. During these agitations, the subjects discussed, the societies organized, and the measures proposed clearly indicate the demoralizing tendency of the principles engaged. Among the disturbing elements most active on those occasions was the doctrine of *equality*. Under its inspiration, clubs were instituted for the promotion of "Women's Rights," the objects of which were to emancipate woman from her subordination to man, and to elevate that fragile sex to an equality with the lords of creation. According to the arrangements proposed, she was to enjoy not only a domestic but a political equality as well; to be released from all the restraints and obligations imposed by connubial vows; to choose the fathers of her children, and to have as many fathers for them as she had children, if she so desired; to be eligible to all political offices; and to vote at all political elections.

In their many earnest discussions of this subject, those social agitators seem to have demonstrated, satisfactorily at least to their own minds, the natural equality of woman to man, without considering the difference of her organization, and the different social duties (that of maternity, for instance) which that organization imposed upon the sex. The ludicrous absurdity of their contemplated reform seems never to have disturbed the complacency of their thoughts, or to have raised a doubt of the practicability of their plans. They do not appear to have asked themselves the questions: What was to be done with a Speaker of the House, or a Presidentess of the Senate, in the seventh month of her pregnancy? or a General-in-Chief, who, at the opening of a campaign, was "doing as well as could be expected"? or a Chief Justice with twins? Or, it might not unfrequently happen that, at periods of high political excitement and closely contested elections, many important voters would be "in the straw" and unable to attend the polls, or, in their zeal for the cause, might go out too soon and bring on serious complaints, to the great discomfort of families and the derangement of domestic order.

The institutions of marriage and the family, and the rights of property, have been vehemently assailed by large numbers of persons known as "Socialists" and "Free Lovers." These frantic and licentious persons, embracing equal numbers of both sexes, attempted reductions of their ideas to practice by forming extensive organizations for that purpose. So far have these speculations penetrated into social life, that, as Comte remarks of the democratic period of French society, any one is now at liberty in the large communities of the North to make an easy merit of the most turbulent passions; so that, if such license could last, insatiable stomachs might at length get to pride themselves on their own voracity.

True, these are but small irregularities, symptomatic diseases, appearing on the surface of society, and no serious evil has yet arisen from them, as they have hitherto been confined to the large metropolitan cities. But they are premonitions of morbid tendencies, shadows cast before of coming events; and those seething caldrons, the great commercial capitals, wherein are commingled, like the "hell-broth" of Macbeth's witches, all the worst elements of our social system, cannot forever confine the ebullition within their own limits. They are legitimate derivatives of the democratic principles, and are chiefly valuable as affording examples on a small scale of events which must take place on a large scale, when society is ripe for their development.

But even if these minor disturbances be regarded as examples of failure to pervert the democratic polity to purposes of evil, it cannot be denied that the dogma of equality has been more fatally successful in another direction. Large numbers of persons in this country became so transported with the apparent success of the democratic polity here, that from being at first only the champions of their own rights, they passed at length into propagandists, and entertained the *project* of carrying the democratic faith over the whole earth. They made no distinction of races; *all men are created free and equal.* But before going abroad, they must establish the universality of the faith at home, and make it a unit here. Four millions of Africans were held in bondage in this "land of liberty:" these Africans were their brothers and equals.

It was precisely here the dogma of equality, aided by the doctrines of free inquiry and popular sovereignty,

wrought with fatal effect. The ruling majority was at the North; the Africans were at the South. No Northern interest was supposed to be compromised by such an application of the equality principle. Indeed, the principle, to be consistent, could not refuse to elevate that down-trodden race to the level of the Caucasian and of liberty at the sacrifice of any interest. The masses, to whom the appeal was made, and who controlled the ballot-box, listened with growing approval. There was law and gospel for the doctrine; for, according to the Bible, we are all descendants of Adam and Eve; and the new Evangel of liberty and politics, the Declaration of Independence, makes them our equals and free by the legacy of birth. Clearly, therefore, we had no more right to enslave the Africans than the Africans had to enslave us. The burning sun of their native clime had blackened their skins; underneath the cuticle, they were, like ourselves, Caucasians, and children of Adam. Not only a common humanity, but a common parentage, united us all. Common justice, therefore, as well as common decency, demanded that the common rights of humanity be extended to these oppressed brothers and sisters. Like ourselves, they had souls to be saved; their souls at least were white, if their skins were black. In heaven they would be our equals,—why not here? In slavery, their intellectual powers were repressed; in freedom, what Washingtons and Newtons and Shakspeares might not issue from this reviled race! "Was not Hannibal," said one speaker, "an African, and Scipio Africanus another?" In any case, our flag, which was *par excellence* the banner of liberty, should no longer float over four millions of slaves.

Aside from all philanthropic, religious, or metaphysical considerations, the masses had a direct interest in this view of the question. They were laborers, and labor itself was degraded by the degradation of their brother African colaborers. Nay, more; the laboring population was increasing, by immigration and generation, at a rapid rate in this country. Within the memory of living men, the population had grown from three to thirty millions—the laboring portion of that increase being disproportionately great. With augmented facilities for immigration, and an enlarged basis for generation, what would it not do within the period of another lifetime! Wages were already being disadvantageously influenced by the increasing numbers of laborers. Capital was beginning, in this country, as in the overcrowded States of Europe, to control and oppress labor. The competition of four millions of slaves was no inconsiderable item in the economical view of the question. Emancipation would speedily remove this competition. Have not the negroes, liberated little more than a half century ago, entirely disappeared from the Northern States? There is no reason to believe that, unprotected by their masters, they would last any longer in the South by the side of white laborers. All experience proves that no inferior race can long coexist in freedom by the side of a superior race. The Indians of this continent were unable to endure the presence of the "pale faces," and have vanished before them. The natives of the Pacific islands are decreasing inversely as the Europeans increase there. The negro, left to himself, will do likewise, and disappear in the same way. In a state of slavery in the South, the negroes have multiplied, by generation, largely in advance of the whites; while, in a state of liberty at the North, their numbers have diminished almost to the point of extinction. At this ratio of increase as slaves, before many generations more they will monopolize the best portions of the continent.

This is a specimen of the argument employed by fanaticism in defense of universal equality. By this summary it will be seen how effectually the argument, when run out, destroys itself; the premises perish in the conclusion, and the heresies of fanaticism are exploded by the inexorable laws of statistics. It is difficult to reason logically and consistently against the truth: the argument sets out to prove the equality of all men, and ends by establishing a general inequality of all men; for it demonstrates that there are superior and inferior races, and that negroes are so well adapted to slavery that it is clearly their normal condition, and contains the only terms on which they can coexist with the whites in this country. The dictates of humanity, therefore, as well as the dictates of reason, would seem to authorize their continuance in the only state in which their existence can be preserved. It will also be seen, by the foregoing summary of its arguments, with what rapidity and ease this species of fanaticism, beginning in purely philanthropic motives, glides into calculations of interest and self-aggrandizement.

All vague notions of public good, degenerating into an indistinct philanthropy, must succumb at last, as we have just seen, to the energetic forces of a highly stimulated selfishness. A humane desire to emancipate the negro, combined with the patriotic purpose of benefiting the country by substituting free for slave labor, may have been the first impelling motive of the abolition movement. But a party begun upon those principles, and expanding into a controlling majority, would not long confine itself to the narrow basis of its first organization. In the confidence of power, and consequent enlargement of views, benevolent and patriotic designs would in time come to be so far displaced by ideas of self-interest, that the very worst perversions of which the former were capable would be unhesitatingly used for the aggrandizement of the latter.

The social malady must be very serious when all manner of persons, however inferior their intelligence, and however unprepared, are stimulated, in the highest manner, and from day to day, to cut the knot of the most intricate political questions, without any guidance or restraint. A licentious freedom of individual minds, such as this state of things indicates, is necessarily hostile to all true social order; for the great political rules which should become habitual guides in determining problems of that character, cannot be surrendered to the capricious decision of an ignorant multitude without losing their efficacy.

To all those philanthropic, religious, metaphysical, and economical views of the abolitionists, the simple and obvious reply was, that the Africans were slaves, so recognized by the constitution, and that the rights of property in them were guaranteed to the owners by the most solemn provisions of that instrument. In the view of abolitionism, this was a very silly replication, since it was opposed to the commonest dictates of philanthropy and patriotism, intensified by the strongest motives of self-interest; and no constitution was entitled to respect which supports such an anomalous and abnormal state of society. From the very nature of things, these views were necessarily partial and sectional, since they were entertained, in a section of our common country where no slaves existed, by a set of persons whose interests were supposed to be injuriously affected by slavery, in opposition to the interests of another section, where slavery legally and constitutionally existed. It is clear, however, that if those views, partial, sectional, and unconstitutional as they might be, should ever come to be entertained by a majority of voters, the constitution, in the respect of that matter, would be obliged to give way to the will of such a majority. From the very nature of things again, those views must necessarily, in process of time, take possession of a majority of the voters of the nation, because the numerical preponderance of the voting population was already very large in the section where there were no slaves; and the numerical proportion of the voters of that section whose interests were adverse to slavery was largely in advance of the number of those who were, to say the most and the least of them, indifferent on the subject. This relative position of the populations of the two sections, large as was already the disproportion of numbers in favor of the non-slaveholding section, was not stationary, but the preponderance at the North was continually growing larger and larger, and the increase was mainly in that class which was hostile to the institution of the South. It is not alone on the subject of slavery that this majority might declare itself in opposition to the constitution. There are many other subjects equally calculated to call forth similar manifestations. The tariff once possessed and exercised this influence, and may do so again. Instead of two, the country has now many sectional divisions, the interests of each differing widely from the interests of the others. Sectional and party majorities may at any time be hostilely arrayed against any one of these, and the constitution be again unable to protect the minority.

Thus it is apparent that the tendency of this government is to run into a government of party; and, from the geographical divisions of the country, the ruling party must necessarily be also a sectional party. This arrangement would seem to be partial and antisocial enough for all the worst purposes of despotism or anarchy; but it is not yet the worst: the ruling party must also be a class party, and that class must consist of the most inferior and least intelligent portion of the nation's population; for, under the rule of universal suffrage, the majority is unavoidably composed of the lowest classes of society, the masses, animated by the most knavish, the demagogues. In the long run, a government thus constituted cannot be otherwise than oppressive. The tyranny of such a majority is, of all others, the most odious and intolerable, because irresponsible. Like the pestilence that walketh in darkness, we feel its effects, but it is invisible, intangible, and no man can question it or call it to account. It has no head to be chopped off, like Charles I. or Louis XVIII.; it cannot be captured and imprisoned, like Napoleon; or expelled the country, like Louis Philippe. It is without a local habitation or a name: it is everywhere in general, and nowhere in particular. Scattered, like the leaves of the Sibyl, over the broad surface of the land, its decrees are gathered up at stated intervals, and contain the fate of the nation. On those occasions, it is the ballot-box that, like the Lion of St. Mark's, opens its mysterious jaws; and if the confiscation of four billions of dollars' worth of property issue thence, why—it was the ballot-box that did it. If it were possible to conceive of an organized tyranny like this as being irremediable, society must perish, and men, like brutes, wander in a state of nature.

This *tendency* of our government to become a government of *party*, and of the dominant party to become a *sectional* and *class* party, has been fully *realized*. The majority which determined the Presidential election of 1860 was nothing more than a party and sectional organization. It had in it nothing of that broad, general, and impartial character which should distinguish the government of a great nation. Its object was not to reconcile conflicting interests, to harmonize political diversities, or unite social divergencies and govern all with equal justice. The dominant majority was organized exclusively at the North; and was composed of a class of persons, the most inferior there, whose social ideas were so peculiar and so partial that they had nothing of general politics in them. The sole purpose of one of the constituent elements of that majority was, as its name indicates, to actualize or carry into practice the abolition sentiments and arguments contained in the above summary which I have made of them. It is not conceivable that this lawless purpose could ever have been peaceably accomplished, since it amounted to an assault upon the rights and interests of another large section of the common country. Nor indeed is it certain that, under a wise and judicious system of resistance, legally and constitutionally conducted, it could ever have been accomplished at all. But a wise and judicious system of resistance, legally and constitutionally conducted, was precisely such a system of resistance as, under the circumstances, was not at all likely to have been adopted; for the same disorganizing principles which influenced the conduct of one party equally influenced the conduct of the opposite party. But this is not the place to exhibit the operation of this double influence. Hereafter, the conduct of the South, and the method of resistance she saw proper to adopt, will be noticed in their appropriate place. It will then be seen that the democratic principles have directed their disorganizing influences with equal force upon both sections; and that, until human nature be changed, those principles, in their present naked form, are unfit to preside over a great and complicated society like this.

I have now completed the analysis which I proposed to make of the democratic polity, by separating its dogmas and treating each by itself. This analysis has revealed the theoretical and practical tendency to excess which is inherent in each dogma; and it will be seen that, when brought together in a state of combination, so far from counteracting or neutralizing the vicious tendencies of each other, their union does in reality augment the evil many times over; for, in point of fact, either of those dogmas would be comparatively harmless without the other two. I shall next proceed to examine the influence which is exercised by the democratic polity over society; and this examination I shall conduct by decomposing the latter into its different social elements, and showing how each element is affected by being brought under the exclusive domination of the former. To this end it becomes necessary, first of all, to go to the basis of the social system, and examine into the nature and extent of the injury, if any, which democracy may have inflicted upon society.

III. Public Morals.

As public morality is the foundation of society, if that be rotten, the superstructure cannot be secure. The first thing, then, which this examination discloses to us, as a peculiar feature of our social system, is the unusual number of public offices, and the still larger number of persons that, in every community, are hanging around to fill them. Many of these offices are created for no other purpose than to reward partisan zeal at the expense of the public purse. The effect of this measure, as unwise as it is wicked, is twofold: it increases venality in proportion to the increase of offices; and it withdraws from the useful occupations of life an extraordinary number of persons that otherwise might be employed in a manner beneficial to themselves and to society, but who, thus converted into vagabonds and loafers, become nuisances to themselves and to the communities they infest. The number of office-seekers bears an undue proportion to the number of offices to be filled. For every successful applicant there are at least a dozen disappointed ones. Society thus becomes filled with crowds of discontented individuals, whose disappointment must awaken passions anything but favorable to public tranquillity. During legislative sessions, many of these office-seekers and ex-office-holders constitute themselves "Lobby members," as they are called; there are always more such members in the galleries than there are legally elected members in the halls of legislation, and their business there is nothing else but organized corruption.

Our frequent elections are the peculiar fruits of the democratic polity. The pretext for their frequency is that the doctrine of *accountability* may thereby be rendered as practical and efficacious as possible. It is pretended that it is only thus the people are enabled to keep a firm hold on the fidelity of their agents. Upon the principle that short accounts make long friends, public servants are required to give an account of their stewardship at short intervals, in order that the people may have the opportunity, as often as possible, of passing judgment upon their conduct; of continuing them in office if their conduct be approved, or discontinuing them if disapproved. This reason would be a very sufficient one if it were always carried out, or even pretty generally acted upon. But these frequent elections, whatever may have been the *theory* of their origin, are *practically* not the least of the social evils of which we have to complain. They are indeed the peculiar delight of democracy, as it is only by and through them it exercises its power over society. That polity would be shorn of much of its capacity for evil, and society would be much more tranquil, if elections were much less frequent. As the people are of opinion that the government is little else than an organ of their will: that it was designed mainly to manifest their power: that, in short, it is *par excellence* "the people's government," as contradistinguished from all other governments antecedent and cotemporaneous; and as they are taught, and do believe, that every man in society has the right and the capacity to fill any office in government, they think that every man should have his turn at some office or other. Hence the doctrine of *rotation in office* has ever been a favorite dogma with the people, and perhaps is quite as responsible for the frequency of elections as the doctrine of official *accountability*. In any case, whichever doctrine may bear the responsibility, it too often happens that public functionaries have scarcely had time to learn the A B C of their duties before they are displaced by other neophytes, and these again by other novices, before any of them could prepare themselves for usefulness in their offices.

The political hatreds and heats of contest engendered at these repeated elections by party rancors, cannot fail to pass into personal and private animosities. Many a quarrel that had no other origin has been quenched in blood; and the peace of families and the harmony of neighborhoods have been destroyed forever by political differences of not the slightest moment to society. These demoralizing effects are witnessed in the daily course of our political conflicts, which are correctly spoken of as a kind of warfare; for actual war cannot be more destructive *materially* than they in a moral point of view. In the fury of these conflicts, the most conscientious men habitually upbraid each other with wickedness and folly. Not only individuals, but different sections of the country, hostilely arrayed, denounce each other in epithets the most vile that can be invented by persons ignorant of everything but the use of vulgar language. If one party succeed by an unusual amount, or some extraordinary method, of corruption, the opposing party, after heaping upon its rival the most unmeasured abuse for such practices, is sure, at a subsequent election, to profit by the lesson, and so far follow the example as to exceed if possible the corruption by which it was previously defeated.

On every serious occasion, at the polls and at public gatherings, doctrines the most opposite are maintained with equal warmth by persons equally entitled to confidence; and in the heat of debate, no extremity is too absurd for their conclusions to be pushed. The greatest strain a principle will bear is always put upon it, not only in argument, but in practice. *Pot-house politicians*, usually a contemptuous epithet in other countries, are here too often the actual legislators; for that class of persons are usually the most successful canvassers, and carry a majority of elections. Wealth, learning, and respectability are almost entirely excluded from legislative seats: the cry of "aristocrat" generally suffices to defeat any man possessing a claim to either of those qualifications. In the halls of legislation, log-rolling, as it is called, is the necessary consequence of such legislators: there is scarcely any local or personal legislation, however glaringly corrupt, but can be secured upon this reciprocity principle. "You help me, and I'll help you," is a maxim of political wisdom soon learnt; and he is the best politician and the most successful statesman who succeeds best with it. Another pernicious consequence of this anomalous state of things is the multiplication of laws beyond all human necessities: many of them become dead letters at the moment of their enactment, and few have ever any attention paid to them. If one of these *parvenu* legislators can point his constituents to a law which he has originated and carried through, he passes for a Solon, and his return at the next election is rendered almost certain. Every "fellow," therefore, must have his law to parade, or he is "nobody," and may expect to be retired by his constituents to the shades of private life.

Among the many evil practices peculiar to our social system, the bestowal of *official patronage*, as rewards for partisan services, stands pre-eminent. This patronage begins at the highest office of the government, and descends to the lowest. The people are not slow to imitate this example; they practice the same thing at the ballot-box with a rigor that is absolutely merciless. Patronage is reduced to a system: it is used as the patrimony of party: every office is a largess, and must be compensated by service to party. The practice has proceeded to such lengths that none but party hacks can hope for office or patronage; and these are bestowed, not for any fitness on the part of recipients, but rather for their unfitness, since they are notoriously, in a majority of cases, the most idle, worthless, and venal of the nation's population. This *inquisition for spoils* takes place on every change of rulers, and at all primary elections. Viewed in the extent to which it is carried here, it constitutes a species of depravity known to no other government in the world. In all governments, more or less patronage is necessarily bestowed by the Chief Magistrate, and other public functionaries holding under him; but in the exaggerated form in which it obtains here, the habit is peculiar to our social system. In England there are many offices which are now held for life by persons who stand aloof from the strife of parties. These functionaries supply to the State a valuable body of servants who remain unchanged while cabinet after cabinet is formed and dissolved, who instruct every successive minister in his duties, and with whom it is the most sacred point of honor to give true information, sincere advice, and strenuous assistance to their superior for the time being. To the experience, the ability, and the fidelity of this class of men is to be attributed the ease and safety with which the direction of affairs has been many times transferred from tories to whigs, and from whigs to tories.* In this country, no such class of officials exist. As often as the administration is changed, an endless crowd of retainers is liable to be ejected from office, and to be succeeded by a set of new hands entirely ignorant of official duties, and who are liable to be ejected in their turn before they have half learned their business. Servility and corruption, ignorance and incapacity, in every department of government, must be the inevitable effects of such a system.

The practice, whether at primary elections or by office-holders possessing official patronage, amounts to a proscription for opinion's sake, which, while it deprives the country of its best and ablest citizens, drives into the ranks of the dominant party all the base and venal, who

* See Macaulay's History of England.

stickle at no dirty work to earn the rewards due to party attachment. In proportion as the vile and corrupt are drawn into a party, good men are forced out of it, or reduced to inactivity; for if they remain they cannot consent to co-operate with such colleagues. As from the nature of our social system the dominant party must in time, if it does not already, constitute the government, it follows that the nation is in constant danger of being subjected to the rule of the very scum of its population.

"To the victors belong the spoils," has long been a recognized political maxim of the first importance. This principle of claiming a monopoly of office by right of conquest, and of filling all offices, at primary elections, by party organizations and for party aggrandizement, must change, *has already changed*, the purpose of government from its true destination. The tendency of such a system is to elevate party claims above the demands of patriotism; to make party attachments stronger than love of country; to postpone the common weal to personal interests; and to convert the government into a joint-stock concern for the benefit of individuals who control it.

Its evil effects cannot, and do not, stop there. Consequences so deleterious to the public interests, arising from an organization of so partial a nature, cannot be confined to government; they react upon the individuals composing the party; they obliterate, in fact, the very spirit and genius of individuality; they erase the lines and marks which distinguish one individual from another; they destroy everything like independence of thought and action; all men must surrender their own convictions, in order to subserve the interests of party; they must put on the harness of party, and work in party traces; they must conform their thoughts and actions, not to the dictates of their own reason, but to the "usages of party," which is a *Procrustean bed* all must fit at the cost of a mutilation at which human nature shudders: in short, they owe fealty, first of all, to party, which is their patron; and this primary allegiance leaves little room for, if it supersede not altogether, loyalty to country; and *proscription* is the iron rod with which all this party discipline is enforced.

It is not only the individuals who are the active members or servile dependents of party that are thus injuriously affected. It is by these methods the *majority* is procured; and the majority rules not only government but society, not only public life but private life. Such a system, either directly or through an overpowering fear of *public opinion*, which it begets, controls the citizen in his minutest affairs. It regulates his public actions, and dictates his fireside enjoyments; it fetters his speech, and forces opinion itself. All spring and elasticity of thought is destroyed; originality disappears. No one dares whisper his thoughts, till he learns whether they are pleasing to the sovereign majority. An *invisible public* is the master, whose crushing tyranny extends to every relation of life. There is no resistance, for its victims are emasculated by fear. It is treason to doubt the wisdom of the majority.

But the evil consequences of such a system go even further yet, and invade every department of social life. It is the nature of any system to be consistent with itself. If it be established on false principles, it tends unceasingly to develop all the pernicious effects of those principles, and forces everything around it to aid in the development. Under such social conditions, therefore, good men cease to avail themselves of their political privileges; they retire in disgust to the obscurity of private life; they shrink with horror from paying the slightest attention to public affairs; they shun the polls as places of contamination; they regard the ballot-box as a solemn mockery, used only to cloak the designs of a party whose leaders have already predetermined the results to be obtained from it, and elected all their candidates beforehand; they look upon popular elections as mere selfish contests for office; and accordingly they abandon the government to the scramble of the bold, the daring, and the desperate.

Here, then, is formed a party organization, held together by the strongest bands which the vicious part of human nature can supply; that is, by the mercenary ties of self-interest, by the fears of the timid, and by a discipline so severe that nothing but revolution or universal anarchy can break through it. The tyranny of such a system, while it lasts, surpasses the worst despotism on earth; for it crushes the soul and withers the heart—all that is not mechanical is exterminated. The most galling thraldom ever known, it assumes the most dangerous form which modern times can supply; it borrows the badges of freedom, and, under the shape of government by the majority, it imperils all our individual rights, and threatens the very existence of freedom itself. But it cannot endure. With corruption and intimidation as its only guarantees, it must demoralize the nation to the point of actual dissolution, or revolution must snatch it from destruction. Distrust and jealousy, fear and hatred, will conspire against it; and civil war, if nothing else will, must at last square the account by ruin or by rescue.

When this party organization shall have become sectional, as, sooner or later, it is bound to do in a country of such magnitude and varied interests as this, and has seized into its hands the reins of government, and is exercising all its party instincts and party appliances, upon what hypothesis would it be possible to predicate the safety of the Union, except upon the supposition that human nature, in other sections, had abdicated its manhood, or surrendered its passions to abject fear or to the wasting influence of corruption?

As for *freedom of elections*,—the very life-blood of popular governments,—that, like many other free things in this free country, is a *myth*—a pleasant delusion, which, in our distress, it is well enough to cherish—but no such thing exists. I speak not now of the interference of government by its army regulations, but of the ordinary working of the system in times of profound peace. A man cannot be reckoned very free in his election, when a caucus nomination has left him no choice of candidates. A few irresponsible individuals, with no authority for doing so but the warrant of party, have already predetermined his vote, without consulting his wishes; or perhaps, worse still, have presented for his acceptance a man whom, of all others, he would most repudiate, and he is free to vote or not. Nor is even this measure of freedom always allowed him: if he eat the bread of dependence, his choice sometimes lies between eating no bread at all or voting as directed. This species of servitude is not always confined to the poor and needy, or to the humble laborer. Lawyers, physicians, mechanics, all men who are dependent upon public patronage for a livelihood, have sometimes been reached, through their professions, by this all-pervading proscription of party, and forced to submit to party drill, to take their politics according to prescription, and vote to order. A well-disciplined corps of office-holders, scattered all over the country, in every State, county, town, and neighborhood, acting with incredible zeal and union of purpose, use their official stations and their offices to very little purpose other than that of influencing elections, of all grades, from the highest to the lowest. They advise, exhort, solicit friends and partisans to greater exertions in the cause of party; they wheedle, cajole, intimidate, resort to briberies direct and indirect; everything is done, which patronage and power can do, to influence elections, not only in the General government, but in all State governments. No office is too high, none too low, to escape their wondrous activity and their marvelous ubiquity. But the greatest levers for controlling elections are party organizations. In this country of office-seekers and office-holders, there are few men who have not political aspirations of their own. This unfortunate ambition degrades the aspirants at once to the level of the most abject servility. They become the slaves of party, and must obey, without question, its behests. Its nominations, however personally objectionable, command their unqualified support. They are perpetually called upon to electioneer and vote for men against whom, perhaps, their very *gorge* rises in opposition; but they must *bolt* the devil himself, if required to do so; and it is the boast of many that they are fully up to this standard of party drill, and could readily fulfill such a requirement. It is scarcely conceivable that such a state of things could last for any length of time: its tendency is to go from bad to worse, and must kill or be cured.

Nor is it alone *freedom of elections* which is so fatally disturbed by official patronage and party organizations. The FREEDOM OF THE PRESS is no less injuriously affected by the same deleterious influences. A FREE PRESS is very justly considered to be the PALLADIUM of a people's liberties. So highly were its services in this respect rated, that it was the only profession which enjoyed the high distinction of being expressly protected by constitutional enactments. In despotic governments, the press is always effectually muzzled, and speaks only, if it speak at all, at the dictation of the despot. But it may well be asked, if a purchased press is more free than a fettered one? It certainly makes little difference whether the manacles be put on by fear or by favor. A pensioned press can no more speak the truth than an enslaved one. The latter may be silent, and thus become a sort of negative institution, calculated to do no sort of good. But a press, hired to lie and mislead, to slander and traduce, becomes a positive evil, calculated to do infinite mischief. Of the myriad political presses in this country, large numbers of them are the servile organs of party, looking alone to party for support, devoted to its interests, speaking only and always at its dictation, and ready to suppress the truth or pervert it, or lie direct to advance the cause of party. This is the most melancholy prostitution of which the democratic principles have yet been guilty. It is a corruption of the very fountain of light and knowledge; a demoralization of the intelligence of the nation. The effusion of blood and tears which will be required to wash out the stains of this pollution, and to restore humanity and society to their lost integrity, is beyond the power of human calculation. The earnest endeavors of many generations will be needed to repair the damage; and, in the mean time, we can but weep over the mistakes of the past, and invoke an early restoration in the future.

In the midst of so much party rancor, of such personal and sectional hatreds, of such impure motives and corrupt practices, all deep and steady convictions must be rendered totally impossible; and no true political morality can be hoped for, by even the most sanguine disciple of democracy, while this state of things lasts. The inevitable result of such a chronic epidemic is the gradual destruction of the public *morale;* while at the same time the seeds are planted of future strifes, the subjects of which will be debated at the point of the sword and at the cannon's mouth. Precisely such a bloody exchange of ideas is that now being discussed, in tones of thunder, over the broad surface of the land. Whichever way, then, we look at it, politically, morally, or, as we shall hereafter see, religiously, WAR lies like the inevitable excess at the extremity of each view; and the democratic principles, as established in the frame of this society, must be regarded as possessing no capacity for social organization.

PRIVATE MORALS.

If such has been the spread of public demoralization, private morality has fared little better. The latter could only be reached through the destruction of the former: and now, that barrier being broken through, the dissolving action threatens domestic, and even personal morality, which is the necessary foundation of every other. In private life, natural sentiment has far more influence than in public relations. In all that concerns domestic and personal affairs men *think* not so much as they *feel;* and their conduct is much less dependent on current opinions than is the case in public matters. While politics and public opinion, by their ceaseless action and reaction upon each other, produce whirlwinds of passion which are so destructive of public morals, those home interests which cluster about the domestic hearth are protected from the pitiless peltings of the storm without by a kind of household *Lares*, the *genius loci*, which render sacred the roof under which they are sheltered. The fanaticism of politics is little less rabid than the fanaticism of religion. Some of the blackest crimes recorded in history are due to ill-regulated public spirit. Men daily do for their party, for their favorite political schemes, what no inducement on earth could tempt them to do for their individual interests. In their ordinary business relations, they would shudder at the bare thought of committing a fraud which they would perpetrate with exultation on the ballot-box. Their reputation would be ruined forever in the eyes of their fellow-men by the mere suspicion of a crime committed in private life, which, in public relations, would win the applause of a party or of a whole community. In politics, the *end* too often justifies the *means;* and men are apt to overlook the turpitude of the one in the excellence of the other. It is more than probable that all the wealth of France could not have bribed Robespierre to murder for hire one of the thousands whom he murdered from motives of philanthropy. These evil passions and evil practices are seldom carried by men into their family circles: they are usually shaken off at their doors, with the dirt from their feet; or left in the halls, with their overcoats; and they enter the sanctuaries, where are enshrined their household gods, with pure hearts overflowing with tenderness and love. Private morality, therefore, is so far removed from the influence of political institutions, that the principles of the latter must be insidious indeed if they can gain an entrance so far into the human heart as to undermine all those guards which nature has supplied to human conduct.

But the intrusion of individual analysis into those sacred precincts, and the corrosive influence of an unlimited freedom of discussion, could not be prevented by any of those safeguards which nature has thrown around the sanctuary of private life. The supremacy of the individual conscience has greatly aided this intrusion; and the dogma of *universal equality* has suggested such license of sentiment and action as, under better auspices, would cause the pure soul to shudder with horror, and would paint the modest cheek with blushes. There have not been wanting pretended reformers who have even denied the propriety of a subjugation of the passions to reason; and have proposed, as a fundamental dogma of their regenerated morality, the systematic dominion of the former, which they have striven, not to restrain, but to excite by the strongest stimulants.* They have argued that the passions are the strongest instincts of human nature, and the most powerful incentives of human action; that the former cannot be weakened without at the same time undermining the vigor of the latter; that therefore the passions, in all their impetuosity, were given for great, wise, and good purposes; and that, so far from emasculating humanity, and reducing it to a cold and passionless machine by their systematic suppression, or by their subordination to the mechanical influences of an impersonal reason, the passions ought rather to be encouraged by a habitual indulgence of even their wildest desires. In the gratification of those desires, it was further argued that the individual conscience must be left as the sole judge and arbiter of the motives influencing individual conduct; and that it is the worst of tyrannies for one person, or for any number of persons, to impose upon others their conceptions of right and wrong: that one person is as much entitled to his opinions as another or as any number of others: that, as all have been left free to choose their own religious and philosophical ideas, so, in like manner, all ought to be left to an equally free choice of their code of moral rules. It will thus be seen that political corruption and moral corruption have, so far, ran together in parallel lines; and that this doctrine is in exact conformity with the right of individual judgment, first asserted by Mr.

* See Comte's Positive Philosophy.

Jefferson, then repeated by President Jackson, and acted on by South Carolina, and again repeated and re-enacted, until, descending through many minor channels, public and private, it finally contributed its quota to the swelling tide of causes which culminated in actual revolution. Guided by the rules of this moral code, the numberless *isms* which, under the name of social reforms, have for years past ruffled the surface of Northern societies, have nearly all of them attacked some cherished institution of private life, which was directly compromised by an abrading discussion which brought into question, without the possibility of solution, the commonest duties of everyday life. Some of these have already been mentioned out of their place; but a repetition of them will be pardoned for the sake of regularity.

The desire of sexual intercourse is doubtless the strongest instinct of our animal nature: its licentious gratification, if universally indulged by legal sanction, would render social order a moral impossibility. With what reverence, then, ought we to regard an institution which so directs this passion that, instead of the disorder its license would occasion, the utmost harmony arises from its regulated satisfaction! The institution of MARRIAGE, at the same time that it satisfies and disciplines the most impetuous of our instinctive passions, lays the foundation of another institution no less important. The FAMILY is at once the basis of the social spirit and the germ of the social organization. Families become tribes, and tribes become nations; and the national unity finds its type in the family. So sacred has this institution ever been held, and so natural is the arrangement, that, amid the fiercest revolutionary tumults, the *Family* has always been respected. But it was not to be hoped that, while the democratic spirit was attacking everything else, it should allow these institutions to escape. Social equality, run out to its last extravagances, has assailed both the above institutions; and Marriage and the Family had doubtlessly, long ere since, been endangered by serious innovations, if public decency and private good sense had not, up to this time, interposed to weaken the pernicious effects of democratic excesses. It was even proposed to take from parents the guidance and almost the acquaintance of their children, in order to consign them to the care of society; and to take from children the inheritance of their parents' property accumulated on their behalf. In a moral and domestic point of view, these propositions were as monstrous as the proposals of another set of social reformers, who advised the abolition of money and the recurrence to a state of barter; the destruction of large cities with the view to a restoration of rural innocence; and a fixed rate of wages, and the same rate for every kind of labor. All these recommendations, private and public, had for their object the same end, to wit, the reduction of society and humanity to a uniform system of the most perfect equality. When, to assaults upon institutions such as Marriage and the Family, we add the attacks of the communists upon the rights of property, and of the abolitionists upon the domestic institution of slavery, with the view of subjecting them also, as all things else, to the inexorable law of equality, such frenzy cannot be regarded other than the most alarming symptom of a tendency to social disorganization. It is no answer to these charges to say that they are nothing else but social eccentricities and individual absurdities, which popular good sense is quite sufficient to restrain; and that the best method to deal with them is to leave them, as heretofore, to the wise reserve of public intelligence, or to the inertia of public indifference, without imposing on society the trouble of providing against them. The sad experience we are now undergoing teaches us better than that. These tendencies are genuine derivatives of the democratic principles, and as such are necessarily progressive as long as those principles are left dominant in society. However feeble may be their first tentative efforts, they will never intermit their energy until they have destroyed either themselves or society by their excesses.

So little attention has been paid to these vagaries, in communities where they were most rife, that their correction has been abandoned to the ridicule of a few humorists, and to the laughter of good-natured people who had little or nothing to lose by their successes. But it was too much to expect that these social reformations, as they were called, at first privately begun, should always or even long confine their activity to the narrow sphere of their origin. The organizations to which they led afforded facilities to political interference too tempting to be resisted. Accordingly, many of them descended to the political arena, and, by adding their passions to the fury of politics, not only complicated but intensified the strife. It is by that means they are enabled to vent their disorganizing influences, and bring about social disturbances which endanger the existence of society. Such was the origin and history of the *Abolition Association;* and from that Association has sprung the *occasion* of our present difficulties. Still do we travel in a vicious circle; and start from what point we will, arrive at last to this inevitable conclusion. Or rather, such is the nature of the disturbing elements of our social organization, that they make everything they touch converge to one point, which is the necessary turn of all social disturbances—WAR.

INFLUENCE OF DEMOCRACY ON RELIGION.

Religion, too, no less than public and private morality, has suffered from the dissolving action of social principles so disorganizing. The attrition of controversial debates, like that authorized by absolute liberty of conscience and the right of free individual inquiry, has worn away the very foundation of true piety, by planting in the hearts of men religious hatred, (of all hatreds the most devilish and infernal,) the rivalries of sects, the anger of church quarrels, the animosities of doctrinal controversies, the spirit of persecution and all uncharitableness, instead of the spirit of peace on earth and good-will to men. How can there be genuine religion without harmony, and how can there be harmony amid the confusion arising from setting up the individual conscience as the sole standard and arbiter of religious truth? A boundless inquiry which leads to no decision, and an endless discussion which eats into the heart and corrodes the soul, are not calculated to produce that tolerance which is the essence of religion, or that benevolence which Christ taught from the mount, or that forgiveness which he breathed from the cross, or that peace of mind which passes understanding.

The questions which theology perpetually agitates are, by their very nature, indemonstrable. They are the absolute, the essence of things, or some notion which shall be ultimate. But the absolute is inaccessible to human inquiry. Absolute notions admit neither of proof nor of reputation. The essence of things cannot be understood by man; and when he requires it of his reason, he asks more than his reason can give. Man's mind is neither absolute nor infinite, and to expect from it solutions that are so, is to overlook the immutable conditions of human nature. Yet there is nothing for which men are more ready to fly at each other's throats and tear out each other's hearts than for differences of opinion on these impracticable questions, whose discussion can generate no durable convictions nor obtain universal assent. The sole vital principle of Christianity is charity, self-sacrifice, peace, and the forgiveness of injuries. All other questions are but fragments of old, exploded theologies which, floating, like waifs on the current of time, have gathered about it only to obscure it. These antiquated dogmas, dislodged by the friction of ages from system after system, have gravitated toward the living nucleus of Christianity, like the dust of old iron around the magnet's point; and, while they do not constitute any part of its real life, have contrived to attract the lion's share of attention, and to perpetrate all the evils committed in its name. In every age, in every form which religion assumes, in every theological system, these same old questions are forever reproduced: their discussion is perpetually renewed: again and again they reappear to disturb the peace of society, and to set man in deadly feud with his brother man; and they are left as indeterminate at last as at first, in order apparently that they may continue to distract the future as they have distracted the past and the present.

Such were the questions that were set free by the destruction of the Catholic unity, and were thrown, like so many apples of discord, upon the world, to be discussed by every man to his heart's content. Upon the occurrence of that memorable event, Protestantism filled Europe with religious dogmas, with religious sects, with religious wars—wars which desolated the nations and drenched their soil with fratricidal blood. As numerous as are those sects in Europe, they bear no proportion to their numbers in this country, according to population. Comte did not overstate the case when he said there were, in the United States, *hundreds* of religious sects, radically discordant, and incessantly parting off into opinions which are little more than individual, which it is impossible to classify, and which are already becoming implicated with innumerable political differences. These sects are so animated with the old spirit of controversial theology, that they have come to regard each other with a pious hatred which nothing but polemical divinity could suggest. With a morality rather below than above the average standard, they condemn to perdition all who are without the pale of their peculiar system of salvation. The absolute dogmas of their profession, fruitful as they are of debate, are yet insufficient to detain them within the sphere of religion. The misty regions of metaphysics and political ethics have peculiar charms for their divines. Many of the preachers declaim little else than party politics from their pulpits: by mixing up theological and social problems, they give to the latter the hue and coloring of the former; and thus it is that, in this country, political questions are endowed with the dangerous quality of breeding discords and animosities, which nothing else but their association with theology could ever give them. There are few reformatory schemes, however absurd and mischievous they may be, with which this disputatious class of persons is not in some way connected. Breach of unity, division, separation, contention, strife,—these are the motives from which they derive their inspiration. Its wondrous activity no longer absorbed in the great work of decomposing the Catholic unity, Protestantism seems to have turned loose its disorganizing dogmas upon itself and upon society. To set bounds to our passions by reason, to our errors by truth, and to our schisms by charity,—these are the least of its thoughts. Its mission is dissolution, disunion, disorganization. The passions of mankind are the great instruments of its power; these it stimulates by the most inflammatory declamations. The awful terrors of religion, and not the sweet ministrations of divine love, are the themes of its oratory. Its god is a god of wrath, of vengeance, of hatred, and persecution: he sits upon a gloomy throne, with the bolts of Jove in his hands, and a fiery hell yawning at his feet. With these terrors, the poor victims are driven from one excess to another: fear, and the cruelties which fear inspires, drive all sentiments of love and union and harmony from their hearts. The ministers of such a faith are religious demagogues who rule their disciples by their baser passions. Like the political demagogues, they aim at power, influence; and popularity is the food on which they subsist. The spirit of party animates their words and deeds. To be the founder of a sect is the height of their ambition. The more schismatic a doctrine is, the more efficacious it is in accomplishing their selfish ends. It was the spirit of sectarianism that snapped the first cord by which the States were bound together. Religious fanaticism took the initiative in the unhallowed work of dissolution. A separation of the Union was inaugurated by a separation of the churches, North and South. The Catholic unity itself seems not to have been more an object of hatred to Protestantism than the Federal Union of the States; and its disorganizing tendencies were as mercilessly directed toward the latter as they had ever been against the former. It denounced the Federal Union as a league with hell and a compact with the devil. All the infernal enginery of its frightful creed was brought to bear with ruinous effect against its continuance. The vengeance of Heaven and the pains and penalties of eternal damnation were invoked against its supporters. All those bitter hatreds, so native and so peculiar to its gloomy religion, and which it knows so well how to rouse, were called forth, like so many evil spirits, to breed discord and disunion. Its pharisaical purity, which is more cruel and proscriptive than the blackest iniquity of earth, was foremost in the van of disturbing causes. It is worthy of notice that those Protestant sects which are most schismatic, which are most intensely Protestant, which no organization can retain, and which are continually sloughing off into isolated parties as individual as their extreme selfishness can make them,—those were the sects which were most active in promoting the work of decomposition which has at last been accomplished. They left no means untried to sow dissension in the minds of men—goodly fields indeed for religious culture, but the worst husbandry which religion ever practiced. They preached treason. They exhorted rebellion. They allied themselves with whatever political or social reforms were most likely to create dissidencies. It was the preachers, not of these sects alone, but of most other Protestant sects, who took in hand the *abolition* doctrine, and made it a religious thesis; and, under that banner, it was they, more than all other agencies combined, that contributed to precipitate the present crisis.

IV. State Rights.

It now remains to consider the influence of the democratic doctrines on *international relations*, and see how they affect the action of the individual States toward the general government. It seems to me that, in this connection, they are not less disorganizing than in the case of individuals. They will be found, I think, on very slight examination, to have given rise to the idea of *national independence*, which is but another name for *national isolation*. In this country the same thing is called *State sovereignty*, whence is derived the doctrine of *State rights*, which has played so important a part in the political history of this nation, and which has contributed its quota to the present complication of our national affairs. To understand aright this doctrine, and to comprehend clearly its influence on American politics, it will be necessary to trace it to its European origin, and connect it with the rise of the democratic polity in the sixteenth century. The rôle it has enacted on the political stage of America will be found to differ very little from its performance in the mother country.

Perhaps the most natural, certainly the most useful, function of the papal power was that from the exercise of which was derived the *unity* which was imparted to the civilization of the Christian era. During the long period of its reign, the Catholic Church maintained a regulating authority over the principalities of Christendom, which extended not only to their spiritual but to their temporal interests as well. It was solely by this means that all Europe was banded together in one great family of nations, and an intellectual convergence established, of which the present European civilization is the last and highest expression. Instead of a Greek civilization, and a Roman civilization, and a variety of other civilizations,—which diversity of civilizations was the fatal idiosyncrasy of the Greco-Roman epoch,—Europe has now *one* civilization, which, from its singleness of design and unity of development, is fast harmonizing the moral discrepancies of the world. This beneficent arrangement—brought about by the stern exercise of a power deemed at the time outrageously oppressive—promises to unite the human race in one grand political combination, wherein will still be preserved national individualities, to the *partial* exclusion at least of those international hostilities which spring from the radical contrarieties of discrepant races, intensified and madly directed against each other by the social prejudices of a different development or a different civilization.

When the papal authority was politically annulled,

the dissolution of European order followed spontaneously from the principle of liberty of conscience. The work of decomposition once begun, there seemed to be no end to the process. The nations wheeled off into separate orbits; owned no common center of attraction; asserted their absolute independence of all external sovereignty; nor would allow the least outside interference from any quarter. Then began the doctrine of national isolation, and mutual non-intervention, so rigidly and jealously enforced up to this hour. Then began also the desolating wars which, for more than two hundred years, depopulated Europe and retarded so fatally her national prosperity. There was no power resident on the earth that could interpose its authority or good offices to arrest these suicidal conflicts; and the combatants were only parted by mutual exhaustion. Religion shared the same disorganization: from the bosom of Protestantism issued innumerable Christian sects, as radically discordant as the nations, whose wars they aggravated, and added their own peculiar strifes to the general uproar.

Luckily for the fortunes of Europe at this crisis of her fate, a compensating movement had already set in, some two hundred years before, which had steadily progressed, and was still progressing, at the expense of feudalism and the Free Cities. That system yielded itself a prey to royalty, and was gradually absorbed into the great empires that rose upon its ruins. Thus while European order was being destroyed, and the nations were without co-ordination and without unity, a recomposition of a different kind was going on, which so aggrandized the nations and occupied their attention that the former process was rendered comparatively harmless.

But now, while all the material agencies, so active in this age, are daily assimilating the nations more and more, and preparing them for broader and more regular associations, this spirit of national isolation, if allowed to continue and be carried out to its utmost latitude, would return mankind to the condition of the middle ages. It is only by a growing concentration of political action that the increasing anarchy of the time can be arrested. For this purpose, a subordination of the secondary to the principal political centers is needed. But the tendency of national independence or national isolation is toward the greatest possible distribution of centers; and if the tendency be unrestricted, the process would be carried on until the ruinous dispersion would so far dissipate all political co-ordination that a complete dislocation of society would ensue, the decompositions of feudalisms would be repeated, and the wars of antiquity would be renewed.

I do not pretend to say that it is even possible for such a condition of things ever to recur. Happily the nature of modern civilization saves us from the danger; and history never repeats itself, or turns back in its old channels. I am only designating the tendency of those principles, and pointing out the difficulties toward which they will precipitate society unawares, unless they be checked by the introduction of some countervailing principle which will balance without destroying them.

So congenial with the military spirit is the democratic polity, that any pretext will serve it for indulging its warlike propensities. The first direct effects of the revolutionary movement begun under its auspices, were the almost interminable wars which, during that epoch, desolated Europe, and extruded from the nations all political co-ordination. Proof of this warlike tendency is seen, even at this day, in the respect paid by the common people to the memory of Napoleon Bonaparte, who, of all men, wasted the greatest amount of power in efforts to restore the military system. It was during the progress of this enormous expenditure of strength, so wastefully applied, that the nations of Europe at last saw the dangers to be apprehended from the dogmas of independence and isolation, which they had so greedily adopted from the start. But so jealous were these dogmas, and so strong was the tendency to isolation, that the continental nations could scarcely be bribed by the subsidies of England to coalesce for their own protection. If it had not been for the policy of non-intervention, and the absence of every principle of political order by which some sort of European unity could be established, the French nation, under Napoleon Bonaparte, never could have plunged the world into such disastrous wars, nor have threatened the obliteration of national boundaries on the continent. As it was, the political map of Europe was, at one time, in danger of being so altered that the military genius of a single individual seemed not inadequate to the task of effacing the work of near two thousand years. The danger, indeed, seems not to have passed entirely away yet. Such a catastrophe is by no means improbable, even at this day. The uneasiness of the nations at every movement of France, and particularly at the restoration of the Napoleonic dynasty, is evidence that some such fears are entertained. It was to avert these dangers, and to restore some sort of co-ordination, some sort of European order or confederation, some regulating authority, or centralized force, that the five principal powers entered into that singular league, of which we have since heard so much, known as the Holy Alliance.

In this country, the same tendency to independence and isolation manifested itself at a very early period. The dogma of State sovereignty was warmly advocated, and was recognized with little opposition at the very inception of the government; and the doctrine of State rights has ever since contributed not a little to the political disturbances of the nation.

The spirit of State sovereignty, as manifested in this country, is identical with the spirit which, after the dissolution of the papal authority, separated the nations of Europe into isolated States. This isolation was so unnatural, so abnormal, so lawless, that it was unreasonable to suppose so many independent States could coexist by the side of each other without conflicts. The nations of Christendom, clustered together in Europe, belong to a single system of civilization. The abrogation of the papal power left no centripetal force to that civilization. It was like withdrawing the sun from the center of the solar system. No doubt the government of the Vatican had ceased to answer the purpose which it was so well calculated to subserve at the beginning, and that its removal had become a work of imperious necessity. But the first consequence of its abrogation was a wild confusion which threw the different members of the system, like so many orbless planets, into collisions which, for a time, seemed to threaten their existence. It turned out in the end, however, as we have just seen, that those very collisions which, at the moment, appeared to be so disastrous, were the means of developing the hidden unity which all the time lay beneath the differences presented by the actual spectacle of Europe in that hour of confusion. And thus, out of the chaos and universal anarchy in which Europe was enveloped, arose the first feeble beginning of a European order, a common center of attraction, around which all the nations of Christendom are destined to gravitate, each revolving in an orbit of its own, obeying one impulse, moving steadily to one end, which is yet unknown, and which no nation has yet reached. In Europe, the occasions which led to the abrogation of the papal power were the crushing weight of its despotism, the severity of its unity, and the frightful abuses of its authority. In America, everything is reversed: the causes which are likely to result in the total or partial destruction of State sovereignty and its derivative, State rights, are the absence of a sufficient gravitating power in the central government, the want of unity enough, the ruinous dispersion of political force caused by so many heterogeneous sovereignties, and the growing abuses of too many unrestricted State rights. Europe had to contend against the despotism of a too stringent unity. The United States has to contend against the despotism of too much license, of a lawless and ruinous diversity. It was the democratic principles, in their Protestant or religious form, which, in Europe, abolished the unity of Catholicism, and brought on the dissolution of European order which ensued. It was the same principles, in their political form, which, in the United States, laid the foundation of those democratic dissipations which have resulted in a dissolution of the Federal

Union. In all probability, the latter country will have to undergo calamities not greatly dissimilar or greatly inferior to those experienced by the former, in order to procure such a co-operation of the States as will suffice for the development of a young, growing, and uniform civilization. In any case, such a co-ordination will have to be procured, let it cost what it will.

Theoretically, the federative system appears to be the most simple of all forms of government; but in practice, it has ever been found the most complex, the most difficult of establishment, and the least capable of being rendered efficient. The system, as established in this country, consists in allowing each State to remain entirely sovereign and independent within its own limits; to leave to it all that portion of government which can reside there, or which it can exercise; and to take from it only so much of sovereignty as is indispensable to a general society, in order to carry it to the center of this larger society, and there to embody it under the form of a central government. In this removal of jurisdiction from the States to the General government, the least possible amount of power is conceded by the States, and only this in cases of absolute necessity. The difficulty in this species of government consists in reconciling the amount of independence, or of local liberty, which is left in the States, with the amount of general order or of general submission, which in certain cases is supposed to have been conceded to the central government.*

It is evident from this statement that here is a system

---

* See Guizot's History of Civilization in Europe.

which requires the most advanced stage of civilization of which we can conceive. To render it efficient and durable, the greatest amount of intelligence, of intellectual discipline, a thorough subordination of the passions to reason, an enlightened will, and a high sense of public duty are peremptorily demanded. The reason is plain enough. Nothing can be more conflicting than two sovereignties existing in the same system. The arrangement, indeed, involves a contradiction of terms, and presupposes an absurdity. There can no more be two sovereignties in one nation, than there can be two suns in one system, or two Supreme Beings in one universe. The meaning of sovereignty is *supreme power*. If one thing be *supreme*, there can be nothing else above it, or its equal. If the States be sovereign, the General government cannot be so. If, on the other hand, the States part with the smallest possible degree of power, and acknowledge obedience to any other authority, they are no longer sovereign or independent. Where one sovereignty, so called, limits another pretended sovereignty, neither is sovereign. Nevertheless, each of these pretentious sovereignties will assert its authority, because it has the *name*, and attempt to make practical the *idea* contained in the *word* sovereignty, as against the other or opposing power. The *verbal* imposture helps to magnify the *real* difficulties of the case, which are sufficiently great without it. If to these sovereignties we add the sovereignty of the people and the *supreme authority* of constitutions, we have a system of antagonisms, and not of reciprocating opposites such as we find in nature. To neutralize these antagonisms we have only a *voluntary obedience*, which

13*

must be rendered by so many parties that the chances of a universal or even a general concurrence are almost infinitely diminished. Hence the necessity of those endless reconciliations and mutual concessions which have procured for our system the prenomen of a "*government of compromises.*" In one sense the vocable is a happy one, because so many compromises are needed that there is never a final adjustment, and we must go on compromising and readjusting to the end of the chapter. With a government so complex and embracing so many antagonistic elements, it would be wonderful indeed if, amid the almost infinite variety of interests implicated in a large society like this, some question should not arise, sooner or later, which would refuse to be compromised, and which, adding itself, like the last feather, to all the other causes of disturbance, should not succeed in breaking down a system already burdened beyond its strength. The danger is more or less imminent according as the state of civilization is more or less advanced. If the nation were restricted to a choice population, with a high degree of enlightenment, a strong sense of public duty, of mutual forbearance and self-sacrifice for the sake of general order, such a government might last and succeed well. Because, where a voluntary surrender of individual liberty is concerned, and no adequate means of coercion are provided, the will of man and his free choice must concur in the establishment and maintenance of the system more than in any other. But where the state of civilization is a low one, and the government is confided to an ignorant multitude, who are more influenced by passion than reason, the chances of collision are so greatly multiplied that nothing short of a miracle could procure a long continuance of such a system.

The federative system is not a new form of government, or peculiar to the United States alone. It is not a first experiment, and we are not left in the dark as to its probable action and future destiny. There is at least one example so nearly resembling our own case that we may accept it as an illustration of the system generally, and of what is likely to be its fate here.

It was precisely this kind of government which feudalism attempted to establish in Europe from the tenth to the thirteenth century; and which failed there for the same reasons it is likely to fail here. The principles it rested upon were identical with those on which is based the federative system of the United States. The barons, or great proprietors, claimed to exercise absolute sovereignty each within his own domain, and affected to yield to the suzerain, or to the general assembly of barons, as much power as would suffice to establish a central government for purposes of general order.* The power thus conceded was, like that conceded by the States to the Federal government, of the smallest possible degree; nor was that power ever allowed to be used against themselves without dispute. If a baron was displeased with a decision, he refused to concur in it, and perhaps called in force to resist it. "Force, indeed," says Guizot, "was the only guarantee of right under the feudal system, if force can be called a guarantee. Every law continually had recourse to force to make itself respected or acknowledged. No institutions

* See Guizot's History of Civilization in Europe.

succeeded under it. This was so perfectly felt that institutions were scarcely ever applied to." The baronial courts succeeded no better than our Federal courts. If a judgment was adverse to a party, and he felt himself in a position to resist successfully, the decision could only be enforced by the strong arm; and war generally ensued. It will be seen at a glance how impossible it was to establish permanently a system like this in a world of ignorance and brute passions such as existed at that epoch. As society could not endure in the fragmentary condition into which feudalism had divided it, and no general order could be established, no law of the general government be executed, and no guarantee given but that of force, society must perish or feudalism be destroyed. The latter was accordingly absorbed into the great European empires existing at this day. But it was not without a long series of the most cruel and bloody wars ever waged on the earth, that the feudal system was finally destroyed, and monarchy was left without a rival or an enemy in Europe.

Being in antagonism with ancient order, to eliminate which it was instituted, "the tendency of democracy is to represent all government as being the enemy of society, and the duty of society to be to keep up a perpetual suspicion and vigilance, restricting the activity of government more and more, in order to guard against its encroachments, so as to reduce it at length to mere functions of police, in no way participating in the supreme direction of collective action or social development." An application of this idea in all its completeness has been made by the States to the Federal government. The least degree of power has been doled out by the former to the latter; and even that little has been thought too much, and many efforts have been made to abridge it. In the estimation of State sovereignty, the Federal government should be little else than a sort of fiscal agent, to collect the public money and disburse it at its dictation; to form treaties with foreign powers, without entangling alliances with any; to guard well the commerce of the States; extend the frontiers of the nation,—all under its surveillance, and on the sole condition of its approval. To do this, no standing army worthy the name was allowed to exist, for fear it might be turned against the rights of the States. The navy, though respectable in itself, was efficient for little else than to absorb very successfully five to ten millions of money annually. The distribution of offices, and the disbursement of the national funds, in equal proportions to the different sections and States, constituted themes of perpetual controversy. To dwarf the proportions of the Federal government and to render it as contemptible as possible, salaries scarcely sufficient for a decent support were meted out to the highest officers. Everything served as a pretext to call upon the government to give an account of its stewardship, that it might never lose the sense of its accountability to its thirty odd masters; and the poor thing was badgered and harassed almost out of its life.

All political problems of moment which have come up for solution since the beginning of the national existence, have been mixed up with the doctrine of State rights. That disturbing principle has intruded itself into all elections which have most agitated the country during the last half century, and has intensified their fury by its own jealousies. The great questions of Tariff, National Bank, Internal Improvements by the General government, derived from it whatever political rancor they possessed, and the decisions of them were mainly influenced by its extraordinary energy no less than by its arguments. Its spirit has been to the last degree captious, exacting, and aggressive. It assumed the right to nullify laws of Congress; to interpret the constitution according to its own understanding, which, of course, was according to its own interests or prejudices; and to disregard or respect decisions of the Federal courts, according as those decisions thwarted or favored their own peculiar views.

This spirit was not peculiar to South Carolina alone, or to any particular State or set of States. However the motives might differ, and the arguments be varied, any State, or set of States, was sure to appeal to its own sovereignty whenever its necessities or its interests might seem to require it. Massachusetts, who was deeply interested in a protective tariff, blamed South Carolina for nullifying a law of Congress on that subject, and denounced the doctrine of nullification as a political heresy. When her own passions were roused on a different subject, in which South Carolina was interested, the heresy becomes orthodoxy in her own case, and her allegiance to a higher law impelled her to the vortex of nullification. Thus, between State rights and higher laws, the Federal government was fast becoming a virtual nullity; the dogma of State sovereignty culminated; and anarchy was rapidly taking the place of order. Like the feudal barons, the States, in their relations with the

General government, were beginning to consult only their own interests or consciences; and like feudalism, the independence is likely to perish in its own lawlessness.

The foregoing statement is sufficient to betray the complexity of the federative system, and the difficulty, if not impossibility, in the present state of civilization, of maintaining for any length of time a form of government so difficult of reduction to practice. The same statement will also serve to reveal the intricacy of the political problems which, by the terms of our social system, are removed from the jurisdiction of the choicest intellects, specially prepared by previous training for that purpose, and consigned to the variable and arbitrary decisions of an ignorant and incompetent multitude. And, finally, it will show that such a form of government, while it is sterile of order or of any reliable guarantees, is most fertile of demagogues who, confederate with the masses, and supplied with the boundless resources which the social system affords, could not fail, some time or other, to initiate a catastrophe like the one we are now witnessing.

NULLIFICATION.

It may be objected that the doctrines of *State sovereignty* and *State rights*, and all the collateral inferences flowing from them, are not authorized by the premises from which they are professedly drawn; that they are, in fact, nothing but the sophistries of politics: false deductions from sound principles: the captious arguments of disordered minds: fallacies employed by unprincipled demagogues for their own selfish ends; and that the form of government ought not to be held responsible for the evil consequences they have been made to bring upon the country.

I do not think so. I shall not defend the demagogues from any charge that may be brought against them. That they are capable of any perversions, authorized or unauthorized, and have contributed their quota to the ruin of the country, is but too manifest. I would, if I could, consign them, without benefit of clergy, to the limbo of lost things, and there end their transgressions. But I believe that the theory of State sovereignty, and all its consequences, good or bad, even to this war, are fairly deducible from the principles of democracy: that they are logical corollaries flowing directly from the foundation and structure of the Federal government; and that the Federal constitution, its antecedents, the method of its formation, the principles of which it is composed, and the manner of its adoption, are answerable, not only for the demagogues, but for all the iniquities they have perpetrated.

A vigorous analysis will reduce the real origin of this war to a controversy which was begun in the convention which formed the Federal constitution, and which was bequeathed as a legacy, along with the constitution itself, to subsequent times. In accepting the constitution, we accepted the quarrel it raised; and are now terminating both together in the only way quarrels are wont to be ended. Stated in precise terms, the subject of that controversy was: Whether the government, about to be formed, should be a *strong* government, or a government of *limited powers* only?

It is not my intention to reopen this controversy by

renewing a debate which has already been of so exhaustive a character. Like all political debates in this "free country," with their boundless latitude of inquiry, the discussion of this subject, while it exhausted the arguments *pro* and *con.*, and still repeated itself, seemed destined never to determine anything, or to come to a termination itself. The exasperation of mind consequent upon such endless indecision could not fail, sooner or later, to find a solution of the problems in dispute by a resort to brute force. The transferrence of the discussion, however, to the mouth of the cannon, does not obviate the necessity of knowing precisely what it is we are fighting about. An exact knowledge of this fact, on the contrary, might help us to a speedier decision than would otherwise be reached.

It would be next to impossible to suggest a new argument on either side of this question; and to repeat those which have been employed again and again *ad nauseam*, and to so little purpose, would be a work of supererogation. Indeed, it is now a mere matter of history, and not of argument at all. All I shall do, therefore, will be to state the history of the case, announce the conclusions of arguments, and announce them in such manner that no other demonstration shall be needed but the bare statement of them. Any further verifications which may be required can easily be found lying about all over the legislative, judicial, and political literature of the last two or three generations. It strikes me, however, that these intellectual exuviæ of an age not yet passed belong already to an extinct order of politics, and will hereafter possess very little interest for any one but the philosophic historian or the curious antiquarian. They were great in their day and generation, however, and were the products of the best minds of the country, the intellectual giants of that epoch, as great perhaps as the greatest of any age or nation. I shall repeat none but the conclusions of the choicest of those intellects: if they support not my opinions, then my opinions must fall to the ground.

It is immensely difficult to generalize, within the compass of a few pages, the details of a voluminous and complicated history like this, and render them at the same time intelligible and veracious. Still more difficult is it to present them in the captivating form of a drama, preserving all the dramatic unities, showing the end contained, as it were, in the beginning, and the beginning developing in the end, without losing the thread which runs through all the intermediate parts and connects them together. Nevertheless, such a narrative, appearing in a work like this, where but few pages can be spared to it, must be done up in that way, or be let alone. I deem it essential to a right understanding of my subject, to take some notice of this part of our political history; and therefore, hit or miss, must make the attempt to incorporate it here in a form sufficiently concise as not to occupy too much space, and sufficiently comprehensive as that nothing material shall be left out.

No doubt a very strong government would have resulted from the labors of the convention, if the inclination of its members had been alone consulted. A majority of that assembly was well inclined to a much more imposing form of government than was ultimately adopted. But the patriotism of that body triumphed over its prejudices. The question finally resolved itself into, not "what is best," but "what is attainable." The reason of this was, that no less than *nine* of the thirteen States were required for the adoption of the constitution.

Now, it could not but happen that, in a country of such magnitude, a geographical line would sooner or later be drawn, on one side or other of which the numerical majority would preponderate, and an interest be found, or created, capable of being fostered by partial legislation. This, indeed, was what had already taken place. Near the center of the proposed Union, a line of demarkation, even at that early day, was traced between two clashing interests, whose rival claims were disturbing the harmony of the convention and threatening a disastrous termination to its labors. That line, running east and west, existed *then* just where it does *now*. The journal of the convention testifies of the struggle between those opposing interests. All over its face, we find evidences of their mutual efforts to adjust the basis of representation in such a manner that each would have the most weight on its own side of this great fulcrum, on which the lever of power was to work. Very soon, the necessity of a compromise became apparent to all, or no constitution, no general government, no Union would be established; but things must remain as they were, in their loose order, under the old Confederation. Indeed, so antagonistic was become the conflicting interests that were distracting the convention, that any stronger government was despaired of. A proposition was accordingly made to retain the old Confederacy, and amend its articles with additional grants of power. But this offer was rejected, and the plan of a national government was reconsidered. It was then conceded on all hands, that unless an adjustment of the balance of power on some equitable principle, which favored neither section to the prejudice of the other, was come at, it was clear that the approbation of nine out of the thirteen States could not be procured for the adoption of the constitution. Accordingly such a compromise was attempted, and was thought to have been secured. But this hostility continually broke out afresh, wherever the contending interests of the two sections and the sovereignty of the States were in the least concerned.

At this juncture, no party prenomens had been adopted on either side. The rival factions seem not even to have given to each other nicknames, a custom which is usually practiced on such occasions. But deducing their titles from their principles, or rather from their measures, their most appropriate designations would be *Centralists* and *Anticentralists*. The prevailing party will always choose its own name; and while it selects for itself the most popular appellative it can find, it generally fixes on the other any invidious or reproachful appellation it can invent. The adoption of the constitution was considered as a triumph of the Centralists, inasmuch as the extremists of the other party were rather opposed than otherwise to any other government than that of the old Confederacy, from the inconveniences of which the country was now trying to escape. Elated by this event, the Central party no sooner found itself in the ascendant, than it assumed the popular name of Federal, denouncing its adversary as the Antifederal party. The latter, all the time, complained that they were wronged in this. They said their adversaries desired *consolidation*, while they wished to establish a *league*, (*fœdus*,) and were, therefore, the only true Federalists. But they protested in vain. Their opponents insisted that the constitution established by them was a *true league*, and the *only practicable* league, and that they who had opposed its adoption were *disunionists*, opposed to *any league*, and, therefore, *Anti-federalists;* and so the name stuck to them. By-and-by, the Anticentral party, as I shall continue to call it, acquired so much popular favor as to be allowed to take a name of its own choosing; whereupon it called itself the Republican party. The name of Federalist, having been rendered odious by the unpopular administration of the elder Adams, the Centralists now attempted to get rid of it, by calling themselves National Republicans, which was the most appropriate, indeed the only appropriate name that party ever bore; but their adversaries continued to fling at them, on all occasions, the disgraced name of Federalist as a term of reproach, and as indeed the dirtiest thing that came to hand. The Anticentral party, having borne the name of Republican for more than a quarter of a century, at last, after the election of General Jackson, who came in under the State-Rights' or Anticentral banner, discarded that appellation as not sufficiently indicative of their real sentiments, and assumed one which they thought was more accurately descriptive of their principles, and at the same time most likely to captivate the popular heart: they were henceforth known as the Democratic party. Their opponents again followed their example: as the name of National Republican had been dishonored by

14*

the administration of the younger Adams, as the name of Federal had been, a quarter of a century before, by his father, the elder Adams, the Centralists adopted the name of Whigs, for no other reason than because it was borne by the successful party during the Revolution, and was still held in high esteem. This name, it was thought, would exactly balance, in the popular heart, the name of Democrat, which the Anticentralists had taken, and which proved to be the most attractive cognomen ever borne by any party in this country. But the name of Whig did not suffice to win political battles against the popular cause. Again defeated and broken to pieces under that appellation, the Central party was, for a long time, without any rallying name. Portions of the disrupted party gathered together under the denomination of Native Americans, and were called, derisively, Know-Nothings: in return, they nicknamed their adversaries Loco-Focoes. But the name of Native American, and the principles it covered, identified them too closely with the hateful measures of the elder Adams's administration, and they slowly melted away under that appellative. In the mean time, other fragments of the broken party, gathering recruits from stragglers in every direction, gradually reunited under the designation which the Anticentralists, after bearing it with honor and success during more than a quarter of a century, had at last discarded for the more popular one of Democrat. It was, then, under the honored and successful name of Republicans that the last agglomeration of the dispersed Centralists, made up now of the "All-Sorts," chose to renew their battles; the extreme wing of the party being known by the name of Black Republicans, or Abolitionists. Having won a decisive victory under this denomination, and broken up, not only the Anticentral or Democratic party, but the Union itself, names have again virtually changed into Unionists and Secessionists, which is the nearest approximation yet made to the names I have given to the two parties in the convention. In the matter of names, therefore, the two parties are likely to end where they began; and, in another convention, fight their last great battle under the banners of Centralism and Anticentralism.

I have thus, *in limine*, gone rapidly through the history of party names, for two reasons: first, in order to identify the two parties respectively under all their changes of nomenclature; second, in order to obviate the necessity of again interrupting the narrative of facts by frequent recurrences to this branch of the history. So that now nothing remains but to trace, with equal rapidity, the history of facts as illustrative of the motives of the two parties, and of the quarrel which was first sprung in the convention and continued to this day.

But before proceeding to this history it will first of all be necessary to state succinctly and distinctly what was the real question at issue in the convention. The great trouble was, the difficulty of preserving the balance of power between the Northern and Southern sections of the country. Hence the danger of establishing a common legislature, with any but *very limited powers*. Northern members foresaw that the preponderance of population would be largely in their favor: that the balance of power, therefore, would be on their side; and that, in order to render that power available to Northern interests, the government must be strengthened, and

Congress rendered, like the Parliament of Great Britain, omnipotent, or as nearly so as possible. Southern members were quite aware of all this, and sought to defeat the scheme of the Centralists by weakening the General government, restricting the powers of Congress, and strengthening the rights of the States. Hence the progress of the quarrel to that point where a compromise was deemed necessary, and was thought to have been secured; but the controversy always returned upon the convention, whenever sectional interests or the rights of the States were involved.

As no method of coercion seems to have been devised, or proposed, or even thought of, all the rights claimed by the States were conceded, in order to predispose them to adopt the constitution. No evidence is to be found in the proceedings of the convention, in its debates, in any argument, suggestion, or clause of the constitution, from which it can be inferred that the convention, or any member of it, regarded the several States in any other light than as being perfectly free to accept or reject the constitution at its sovereign will and pleasure. In the event of a rejection by one or more of them, no forcible measure was proposed to meet the emergency. If nine of the States adopted the constitution, then the Union was to embrace those nine. If the others could not be persuaded to come in, they were free to stay out. If nine States did not accept, then the labors of the convention were to go for nothing. It is clear therefore that, at that early day, the convention, and every member of it, and everybody else, considered each State as at liberty to adopt the constitution or not, as it saw fit. If this constitutes sovereignty, then the States were universally believed at that time to be sovereign. Whether or not they lost their sovereignty at a later day, is another question.

The next evidence we have of the *animus* of the convention, and of its opinion of the nature of the government it had formed, is to be found in the method provided for the adoption of the constitution. It was to be adopted, not by a majority of *all* the people of *all* the States, *taken collectively*, as Mr. Webster declared, but by the people of *each* State, each *acting for itself*, in its sovereign capacity. Accordingly, the people of each State did vote *separately*, and not *en masse* with all the people of all the States *collectively*. If this were an act of sovereignty, then the States were sovereign, and believed to be so, up to the moment of entering the Union.

To the same end, when a proposition was made to declare the people of the United States a body politic, or nation, it was rejected, and the very word *nation* and all its synonyms and derivatives were carefully avoided, and were never after allowed to appear in the constitution. The very first proposition adopted by the convention was originally expressed in these words: "That a *national* government ought to be established," etc. When parties were formed and their principles better understood, the word "national" in this sentence became so offensive that it was expunged, and replaced by the words "United States," that is, the several States constituting the Union, or which have united for a specific purpose, and not the United States as a *nation*, or consolidated empire, as Mr. Webster would have it mean. The original preamble of the constitution ran in these words: "We, the people of the States of New Hampshire, Massachusetts," etc., naming all the thirteen States, "do ordain, declare, and establish the following constitution," etc. When the resolution was adopted requiring the approbation of *nine* States to establish the constitution, it was discovered that the preamble and this resolution might come in conflict, and vitiate the whole concern, as it was uncertain whether more than nine would adopt it, and, of the whole thirteen, which of them would constitute the nine; it was therefore agreed to alter the phraseology, and instead of naming each State, to substitute the words "United States." This is the explanation of the phraseology employed in the constitution, of which Mr. Webster made such an improper use, attempting to deduce from it a purpose on the part of the convention to establish a consolidated empire.

All these arrangements were the result, not of accident, but of design. The question of a consolidated government was mooted in the convention, but met with such vigorous opposition from the Southern States, that the project was speedily abandoned. State pride, or rather State sovereignty, taking the alarm at the insidious efforts of Mr. Hamilton, and other Northern members acting with him, to merge the separate State sovereignties into one great central government, set to, with deliberate purpose, to extort an acknowledgment, in one form or other, of their independence, in every provision of the constitution in which it could be decently inserted. In this, the Southern members, joined by no inconsiderable number of Northern delegates, were so successful, that Mr. Hamilton retired in disgust from the convention, and did not resume his seat until toward its close.

So far, then, as the opinion of the convention can be taken as evidence in the case, the States were, in the estimation of that body, not only sovereign before the adoption of the constitution, but that sovereignty was intended, with premeditated design, to be preserved and continued, and was considered to have been effectually preserved and continued, by the terms and provisions of the constitution itself. The State of Rhode Island was the last to ratify the constitution and enter the Union. For a long time it was thought doubtful whether she would do so at all. One of her objections was understood to be this very arrangement, by reason of which, she said, the new Union would be no better than the old Confederation. Rhode Island, in my opinion, was right; and subsequent events have proved that she was so.

And now, at last, all the States having "*acceded*" to the constitutional "*compact*,"—to use Mr. Calhoun's pet phrase,—and the government being in full operation under the Presidency of General Washington, Mr. Hamilton, as Secretary of the Treasury, in connection with other statesmen of his school of politics, including some of the most brilliant intellects of the country, attempted, by means of administrative measures and legislative enactments, to accomplish that which he so signally failed of achieving in the convention. General Knox, one of the adherents of Mr. Hamilton, is understood, on the authority of Mr. Jefferson, to have proposed to General Washington to assume the crown before the army was disbanded, and pledged its support to sustain him in the treason. The virtue of that great man defeated the treacherous design of his Secretary at War; and the Anticentralists, with Mr. Jefferson at their head, defeated all the indirect means of Mr. Hamilton and his friends to centralize the government. The alleged abuse of executive and legislative power during the administration of the elder Adams, who succeeded General Washington in the Presidency, called forth from the Anticentralists the celebrated Kentucky and Virginia Resolutions of 1798–99, drawn up by Mr. Jefferson, in which the doctrine of State interposition, or State veto, or, in plain terms, the right of *nullification*, which is but another term for the right of *secession*, was for the first time plainly enunciated, and became ever after a political formula of that party. But long before that doctrine expanded into actual nullification in South Carolina, several other States were openly manifesting no inconsiderable degree of impatience under Federal rule. An opinion prevailed that if the laws of a State were put into a penal form, Federal jurisdiction could be ousted from the limits of that State, because the State tribunals had an exclusive jurisdiction over penalties and crimes, and it was inferred that no Federal court could wrest the authority from them. According to that principle, the State of Ohio passed the laws taxing the branch of the United States Bank, and high penalties were to be enforced against every person who should attempt to defeat her taxation. The question was tried. Mr. Clay was counsel-at-law to bring suit against the State, and to maintain the Federal authority. The trial took place in the State of Ohio. Judgment went against the State. It was expected that force would be used to resist its execution. Indeed, a most imposing exhibition of force was made. Mr. Clay testifies that he never before in his life saw such a brilliant display of arms and musketry that had been collected for the occasion; but in the end no use was made of them, and the law was allowed to go into execution. In Virginia, a case somewhat similar occurred. Persons were liable to penalties for selling lottery tickets. It was contended that the State tribunals had an exclusive jurisdiction over the subject. The case was brought before the Supreme Court, and decided against the State. Again, in spite of a threat of forcible resistance, the law had its course.*

For a period of a quarter of a century—from the accession to power of Mr. Jefferson in 1801, to the end of Mr. Monroe's second term in 1824—the government was so completely in the hands of the Anticentral party, that the controversy attracted comparatively little attention. Upon the election of J. Q. Adams to the Chief Magistracy of the nation, the quarrel broke out afresh, and was not again allayed until it culminated in actual *nullification*. When, subsequently, a subsidence did take place, the country was still a smouldering volcano, quick with the living fires of revolution, which nothing but blood was destined to quench.

Mr. Adams, during his Presidency, openly espoused the cause of *centralism*. No sooner was he installed in office, than either his folly, or his frankness, prompted him to call upon all the world to note the perfect identity between National Republicanism and old-fashioned Federalism—which were but other names for *centralism*. All the distinguished Federalists of the country came to

* See Mr. Clay's Speech on introducing the Compromise Bill.

his banner. This was the most brilliant epoch of American politics, the Augustan era of her great statesmen. The triumvirate which at that time shed such luster over the debates of the American Senate was perhaps never equaled, certainly never surpassed, by anything of the kind in the world's history. Webster, Clay, and Calhoun constituted a triplication of greatness, in a single department of intellect, occurring at the same time and place, and in such close juxtaposition, which rarely happens anywhere or in any age. They were the bright particular stars of the Senate chamber, and were surrounded by a host of luminaries similar in kind, and scarcely if at all inferior in degree. These intellectual giants met in deadly combat on this theme, which Mr. Adams threw as a bone of contention in their midst.

Since the adoption of the constitution, the old controversy had assumed a somewhat different form: it now turned upon the nature and extent of the powers conferred by the constitution on Congress and the General government. The *Centralists*, or, as they were now called, the *Federalists*, in order to extend the powers of Congress as far, and to as many objects as possible, contended for the largest and most liberal construction of the terms in which every grant of power is couched. The Anticentral party, on the other hand, denied to Congress and the General government every power but what was specifically granted to it; and contended for the most strict and rigid construction of each specific grant. Upon this question, then, issue was joined. As the specific grants of the constitution are so few, the *Centralists* saw that they must fall short of their aim, unless they could establish some principle authorizing a rule of construction which might justify the assumption of powers not named in that instrument, or the extension *ad libitum* of those that are named. To this end, a very cautious beginning was made in 1825. Mr. Adams, in his inaugural address, threw out a *feeler* in the shape of a sneer at all those who could think our forefathers "so ineffably stupid" as to intend to restrain Congress from doing whatever Congress might think it advisable to do. Chancellor Kent, about the same time, declared from his tribunal of authority that, "since 1812, the progress of public opinion had been in favor of a pretty liberal and enlarged construction of the Constitution of the United States." Mr. Chief Justice Jay *suggested* the existence of a Union among the people of this country long anterior to the Revolution, upon the ground that they were all *British subjects*, owing allegiance to *one* monarch; that they were in a strict sense *fellow-subjects*, and in a variety of respects *one people.* Chancellor Kent seized upon this suggestion, and, in his Lectures on the Constitution, asserts roundly "that the association of the American people into one body politic took place while they were colonies of the British empire and owed allegiance to the British crown." This was an unsupported proposition, of which the lecturer made no further use than merely to state it. This proposition, then, which was first suggested by Chief Justice Jay, and put forth, naked and unsupported, by Chancellor Kent, was expanded and enforced, in the most elaborate manner, by Judge Story, in his lectures as Dane Professor of Harvard University. It was finally adopted by Mr. Webster as the principal basis of his arguments on the constitution.

Here, then, was the place "where the wild fig-trees joined the walls of Troy." This was the ground on which the *Centralists* relied to support their broad and liberal constructions of constitutional grants of power, and to extend the legislation of Congress to subjects over which no specific grants of power were given. And here it was that all who would defend the palladium of States' rights must meet the enemy, and fight him back from beneath this cover into the open plains of facts and common sense. Mr. Tazewell and Judge Upshur, of Virginia, met their brother legist in debate, and found it but too easy to demolish the ill-chosen foundation on which that distinguished jurist relied to construct his arguments; and Mr. Calhoun and his allies, I must confess it, were equally successful with Mr. Webster.

During Mr. Adams's Presidential term, which, unlike his immediate predecessors', was not renewed, Mr. Clay was Secretary of State, and Mr. Calhoun was President of the Senate. Neither of those gentlemen, therefore, participated in the unimportant skirmishes which took place in Congress during that administration. This being the first time, for a quarter of a century, that *centralism* had arrived at power, it was deemed but fair to allow it the opportunity, without captious opposition, to unfurl its banner and display its principles. Those principles finally succeeded, at the close of Mr. Adams's single term, in actualizing themselves in the tariff act of 1828, commonly called, by its opponents, the "Bill of Abominations." The passage of this act transferred to General Jackson's administration, which immediately succeeded that of Mr. Adams, the strife which, at that epoch, raged with such fury that it threatened a dissolution of the Union.

The tariff bill of 1828 was evidently and avowedly passed more as a measure of protection than revenue; but as the majority refused to amend the title of the bill, so as to make it appear on the face of it that the duties were laid for protection and not solely for revenue, there was no chance of bringing the case before the courts in order to obtain a judicial decision of its constitutionality. The entire South was very indignant at the passage of a measure which it deemed so unjust and oppressive, and looked to Mr. Calhoun for a solution of the difficulty. That gentleman could see but two possible remedies: one was a repeal or modification of the tariff under the auspices of the incoming administration; the other was what he called State interposition or veto, the naked meaning of which was *nullification*, or still worse, *secession*, or still worse yet, *dissolution of the Union.*

The hope founded on the first of these alternatives proving fallacious, the second alone remained as a *dernier ressort.* Accordingly, South Carolina, with a boldness which partook more of rashness than courage, proceeded, on the 24th day of November, 1832, to pass an ordinance annulling the operation of the tariff law within her limits. Congress convening soon after, the whole subject was placed before the Senate by a Message of the President, which was referred to the Judiciary Committee, who, thereupon, reported the bill which has usually been called the Force Bill. Upon the authority of this bill, the President issued his celebrated Proclamation, and both parties proceeded to make hostile preparations.

At this juncture, the State of Virginia, the most powerful Southern member of the Union, interposed her good offices. She earnestly entreated South Carolina to suspend her ordinance, and appeal once more to the justice of Congress. Thus solicited, South Carolina agreed to suspend measures of forcible resistance until every peaceable means for an adjustment of pending difficulties was exhausted. No express agreement was made by Virginia, but a very strong implication was raised by the method of her interposition, and by the consent of South Carolina, at her solicitation, to defer immediate action, that in the event Congress refused to afford the desired redress, the former State would join her fortunes with those of the latter. It cannot be doubted for one moment, if Congress had denied the justice which was asked, that Virginia would have felt herself bound by every principle of honor, and by every consideration of interest, to make common cause with South Carolina; and if she had done so, it is equally certain that the entire South would have eventually become parties to the contest, and the war, which has been thrown upon the present generation, would have come off then.

Apart from selfish considerations, there are many reasons calculated to raise regrets that such was not the case, since it is morally certain that such a conflict, however it might be deferred, was bound to take place some time or other. At that epoch, the fanaticism and demagogism, which are now monopolizing the counsels of the nation and covering the land with desolation, did not exist. Public life was filled up with so many great men, able statesmen, eminent characters, with broad and liberal views, that their presence and influence would have insured a generous conduct of the war, waged upon lofty principles and in the true spirit of an enlightened and disinterested patriotism. The character of the distinguished military chieftain who then occupied the chair of State would have been a sufficient guarantee against the imbecility, the blunders, and charlatanry which are now protracting the agony of the nation almost to the point of dissolution. Under auspices so favorable, there is scarcely a reasonable doubt that the war would have been a speedy one as well as a generous one; that not alone a flaming sword would have flashed wrath and vengeance over the country, but the olive branch of peace would have gone forth steadily and continuedly with the sword of justice; that power would have been tempered with mercy; and, above all, that no act of ruthless vandalism would have been committed, as has now been done, to put it out of the power of the insurgents to propose terms of capitulation, or even to speak of peace except as humble suppliants on their knees. Under such conditions, there is every reason to believe that much if not all of the private suffering and individual ruin which have been entailed upon persons, many of whom were entirely innocent of the war, would have been avoided. There would then have been nothing in the way of a *cordial* reconstruction of the Union upon a broad and solid foundation, which, perhaps, might have lasted for an indefinite period.

On the other hand, there is no lack of reasons in

favor of things as they are. At that early epoch, the democratic principles had not sufficiently developed themselves: they were not as well understood then as they are now: they had not manifested all their tendency to license, or all their capacity for disorganization; and in all probability a reconstruction might have taken place without those modifications which are now inevitable before a permanent pacification can be effected. So infatuated were this people in favor of the democratic principles, and so little did they know of their real character when unrestricted, that their agency in our troubles seems never to have been suspected. It has been wisely said, That fools rush in, where angels fear to tread; and for real mischief, there is nothing like a set of fools to perpetrate it; all villainies result from a want of sense. It does seem, therefore, that fools and madmen were absolutely demanded for the present crisis, in order to effect an utter demolition of the existing order of things, and clear the way for a future reconstruction of government on principles which shall be self-sustaining and durable.

But to return to our narrative. South Carolina, then, at the instance of Virginia, suspended her Ordinance of Nullification, and made the desired appeal to the justice of Congress. The appeal was not made in vain, for there were intellectual giants in those days, and great men are always liberal, conciliatory, and forbearing. Mr. Clay had ever been the great pacificator of his country's troubles. Conciliation was an office for which his great heart and noble intellect appear to have been peculiarly well adapted. He assisted at the conference which, in 1814–15, negotiated the treaty of peace between England and the United States, at Ghent; he quieted, by compromise, in 1820–24, the difficulties which were precipitating the nation into civil war on the occasion of the admission of Missouri into the Union; and he was not wanting, in the same capacity, on the occasion which had just arisen to call for a fresh display of his compromising tendencies. In the true spirit of a lofty and enlightened patriotism, he now made an unhesitating sacrifice, on the altar of his country's peace, of his own cherished plans, and promptly introduced into the Senate a bill, which ultimately passed both Houses of Congress, called the *Compromise Act.* This Act provided for the gradual reduction of duties on imports, running through nine years, till they were brought down, in 1842, to the revenue standard—a measure which substantially met the views of South Carolina. Her Nullification Ordinance was accordingly withdrawn: the differences, which threatened such melancholy consequences, ceased for the moment; and harmony and peace were apparently restored.

So far, then, neither party seems to have taken or lost anything by this motion. Beneath a treacherous disguise, their real attitudes were but little changed. An apparent tranquillity masked a deadly hostility. The respective principles of the two parties remained pretty much *in statu quo ante bellum.* The question was adjourned, not decided. The combatants drew off with scowling brows. It was a truce, not a treaty: an armistice, not an amicable adjustment. The nullifiers were checked, not mated: they still sent forth their notes of defiance: their curses were not minced or muttered, they were loud and deep: another time they would not be balked. At least something was gained by this ebullition, this cropping out to the surface of a hostility which had lain dormant, but uneasy in its slumbers, during a whole generation. Both banners were at last fairly unfurled: their mottoes flew high in the air: there was no mistaking the question now. Accordingly there succeeded, to this armed and angry pacification, many years of the stormiest politics that ever tried a nation's stability. Under their new name of *Democrats*, and with the powerful aid of Northern allies, the old Anticentral *alias* Republican *alias* States' Rights party succeeded in annihilating, at the ballot-box, the new organization of their ancient enemy, the old Central *alias* Federal *alias* National Republican party, who now, like themselves, fought under a new *alias*, the honored name of *Whigs*, of revolutionary memory. This decisive engagement was again followed by another short period of treacherous tranquillity, and the policy of the government was thought to be settled for all time to come. But again the contest was delayed, not determined. The hostility, indeed, was a radical one: its cause lay at the heart of the nation, in the very roots of the government; and the quarrel was bound to renew itself at each succeeding generation, and, at each renewal, with more deadly purpose. A new occasion must be sought and found, indeed would be sure to present itself, whereon the conflict would at last become one of life and death, a war to the knife and the knife to the hilt.

Looking back at this controversy from the point of view we now occupy, and contemplating it in the form it had acquired in 1832, the first things that strike us are the proportions to which it had grown, the prospective character it had acquired, and the threatening expression of its aspect at that juncture. It was no longer a vague and undefined jumble of puerile abstractions: its sudden and rapid development into the practical measure of NULLIFICATION startles the mind like a clap of thunder. Notwithstanding this Pallas-like form, in which, at a single bound, it sprang all armed from the midst of verbal disquisitions, the quarrel, nevertheless, was no new one, abruptly sprung upon the country on the spur of the moment and without antecedents. Possessing already a past, it now acquired a future. It became a drama of three acts, of which Nullification is the second. That measure is the "middle," of which the "beginning" lies far back in the past, and the "end" as far forward in the future. The *protasis* began in the convention; the *epitasis* was reached in 1832; and the *catastrophe* is now unfolding. Nullification, then, stands, like a double finger-board, half way between the two extremities, pointing in both directions, marking the precise progress the quarrel had made up to that point, and telling as well whence it came as whither it tended.

The moral metempsychosis through which this controversy has passed, from the egg to the fly, from its inception eighty-seven years ago to its *denouement* now enacting, does not differ from the material metamorphoses peculiar to all organized beings. The changes at different epochs are not more violent in the one case than in the other. The Proteus, once declared, was bound to complete the series of transmigrations, possessing still an unbroken identity through many mutations of form, and over long periods of time. The *stages* of its developments are far asunder, but connected by a surprising unity of duration between acts, unity of place, and unity of parties. Individuals, the *dramatis personæ*, change, because at each period a single generation had passed off the stage; but the parties and the motives are identical. The *occasions* of its manifestations are different, the *cause* is always the same. Its *methods* of action vary, its *spirit* is a unit.

In the convention its elements were all rudimental, in a state of envelopment, as it were; but they were all there. In 1832 its elements exhibited a marked development, the quarrel acquired suddenly a vigorous and decided organization, and gave the first indications of its *purpose*, which was as yet feeble and uncertain. In 1861 its *purpose* was fully matured, and realized itself in quick and terrible action. In the convention the *occasion* of its manifestation was of a purely sectional nature, sectional interest; and this continued to be the active motive of the quarrel throughout its whole life; but, beyond its sectional character, the occasion or the motive of the controversy was, in the convention, indefinite, indistinct, without form, and void. The parties merely averred that, from the magnitude and configuration of the country, there would necessarily be one section in which the numerical majority would declare itself in preference to another; and that, in the most populous section, some *interest* would be found, or created, on purpose to be fostered, which would grow by fostering until it dominated every other. What this *interest* might be, was not then known or suspected. In 1832 the *interest* had already actualized itself in the *tariff* of 1828, said to be an oppressive measure, which discriminated in favor of the North against the South. The negro question, as a disturbing element of society, was not yet fairly before the people; but abolitionism, as a social, moral, and religious problem, was already propounded and warmly discussed: it was only in the bud, but promised a robust growth and a foul flowering. In 1861 the tariff, without losing its influence, gave precedence to the question of slavery, which had now passed its bloom and was arrived at its bitter fruitage. In the convention the *method of resistance* was simply to reject the constitution, and leave things where they were. In 1832 the method of resistance was the peaceable remedy of nullification, without *secession.* In 1861 the remedy was *secession*, with *flagrant war.*

Throughout all these mutations, modifications, and developments the real *cause* continued always the same; the *spirit* one and indivisible. The first was sectional jealousy, State sovereignty, State rights, or by whatever other name it may be called. The other was the "spirit of the age," derived from the revolutionary principles already described, which liberated the human mind from the tyranny of the old theological *regime* of the middle ages, and which have ever since taken entire possession not only of the mind of society, but of all individual understandings in this country. This spirit has been greatly intensified by a sense of wild and lawless liberty inherent in the organizations of the people, inherited from their old Scythian ancestors, who, more than a thousand years ago, defied the arms of the Roman world, and finally built empires of their own upon its ruins. This hereditary love of personal freedom, of individual liberty, which the people brought hither, has been so fostered by the physical conditions of the country, by their habits and antecedents, until it has become as anti-social as was the temper of their savage progenitors. It is a natural process to transfer this strong feeling of personal independence to local associations, and thence, by an easy transition, to one's own State, or even section, as opposed to that broader association, or general society, which is too wide to be embraced by one's sympathies, and whose tendency is to obliterate all distinctions both of individuals and States.

PART II.

CONSEQUENCES OF THE WAR.

Geographical and Political Unities of the Nation.

If the views set forth in the foregoing part of this work be at all correct, I think there can be little doubt as to the true genealogy of the present war. That it was already a foregone conclusion of the fundamental dogmas of the government at the moment of its establishment, none but a very common logic has been needed to demonstrate. Assuming, then, that it has been fairly deduced, as an inevitable consequence, from the spirit of our social system, the question occurs: Will the war satisfy that spirit, or quench its disorganizing tendencies in the blood it is now shedding?

Many considerations, based on the passions and the weak side of human nature, would seem to return a negative answer. But every consideration of reason, and justice, and sound policy requires that an instant stop be put to this iniquitous strife, and that the higher claims of humanity and civilization be attended to. The war is so much the more iniquitous because there was so little necessity for it, because indeed it was so purely gratuitous, and because the age has gone by when domestic quarrels were *necessarily* adjusted by such methods.

At an earlier period of the world's history this war might have been allowed to take its course and settle the controversy in its own violent way; and indeed it would have done so without let or hinderance, for the world then knew no other way of settling disputes except by brute force. But now humanity is too far advanced in age to close its ears against the voice of reason, and allow ignorance and brutal passions to take its affairs out of its hands and dispose of them in the manner a set of wild beasts might be supposed to do. The nation which claims to be the advance guard of civilization ought to know better and do better.

In point of fact, there is no necessary antagonism between the northern and southern divisions of the nation of a nature to repel each other. Their present hostility is founded upon a misconception of the true interests of both parties; and a very little reflection will suffice to rectify the errors of ignorance and passion. The geographical configuration of the country predetermines it to a political unity, and points it out as the locality of an empire of the first magnitude among the powers of the earth. Its northern and southern sections, so far from being hostile to the peaceable action of its social relations, are the positive and negative poles of the nation, whose friendly antagonism is essential to a healthy and vigorous exercise of the national functions: they are reciprocating opposites, admirably calculated, by their action and reaction upon each other, to invigorate the national life to a point of intensity never reached before perhaps by any nation.

Owing to its peculiar physical conformation, this country never could have been the nursery of infant communities possessing civilizing instincts. It contains none of those natural divisions, in which Europe is so rich, capable of receiving the first small beginnings of incipient nations, and protecting them against each other until they were able to protect themselves. Europe is an assemblage of just such marked contrasts and bold reliefs, constituting a series of localities so fortified against each other by natural barriers, that each has been a cradle for nurturing, and the theater for bringing forward, a nationality of so much importance to the full development of humanity that the civilization of the world would have been incomplete without it.

Here, on the contrary, the whole country is open and exposed from one extremity to the other, from the Arctic circle to the tropics. The only mountain barrier in it is banished so far to the west as to give it an eastern slope of more than a thousand miles from the Rocky Mountains to the Atlantic Ocean, with no obstacle to overcome in the passage across greater than a few fine rivers of no considerable width. The climate of the United States—though embracing twenty-five degrees of parallel, and including nearly the entire temperate zone of the northern hemisphere on this continent—is so equalized by physical causes and by geographical and astronomical laws as to offer no violent contrasts, nor detract to any appreciable degree from its general character of unity. It would seem, therefore, from these and other causes, that this country was designed to receive a homogeneous people, with a ready-made civilization, who should form a single nation with no moral or social diversities greater than its geographical disparities.

Accordingly, thus summoned, such a people did actually come to it in the fullness of time, with a civilization already prepared, and formed at once a nation of the kind described. As was prefigured by the geographical unity of the place, the population have been in a large degree homogeneous, and have continued the development of the civilization they brought with them in a manner no less uniform and harmonious. Speaking the same language, obeying the same laws, conquering under the same flag, exulting in the same great men, owning the same imperishable history, the inhabitants, from one extremity to the other, have marched forward in a career of civilization with a unanimity of sentiment and design rarely equaled and never surpassed.

With a government adapted to the exigencies of the nation, the small social differences which have grown out of equally slight local diversities need cause no other than a sense of mutual dependence and a desire for the closest relations. Those differences will in fact only serve to excite a more active life, a more extensive and lasting interchange of all that each can give in abundance to its rival. So far from being natural enemies, the two divisions are but too well adapted, too truly made for each other; they have too much need of each other, they are too much the complement of each other, not to unite for their common interest. There is between the two peoples a common basis, an essential, indissoluble tie, which they are not at liberty to break.

But to insure a lasting co-operation of functions, a durable interchange of mutual benefits, requires a perfect equilibrium of political forces between the two sections. The balance once destroyed, a rupture of their peaceable relations is inevitable. Notwithstanding its moral and physical unities, which are very remarkable for a territory of such magnitude, this country is still too large, and its social interests are too diversified, not to give rise to those divergencies of opinions which are sure to find their ultimate solution in war, unless artificial arrangements be employed to reconcile their differences. To preserve this balance of power is the duty of government. If the government be of a kind to excite sectional hostilities instead of allaying them, it is not adapted to the purpose of its creation. The tendency of all social systems is to conform themselves to their moral and physical surroundings. If they be hindered in their destination, or if their spontaneous movement be obstructed, strife, and sometimes ruin, ensues. Our present difficulties are attributable to obstructions which are offered to the spontaneous efforts of society to rectify its incongruities. If for this instinctive movement of society a rational method of development be substituted, the inevitable confusions of the former may be obviated, and the desired reforms be obtained by the peaceable means of the latter. The first step to this end is to ascertain the cause of disturbance. A class of persons at the North, respectable for its numbers, believes the disorganizing element is to be found in Southern society. The people of the South, on the contrary, are of opinion that the cause of disturbance is exclusively at the North. The object of this work is to locate the evil in the fundamental principles of the government, which, acting equally upon both sections, have become obstructive to peaceable relations and to social order. As we have already, in the first part of this work, had a glimpse of Northern society, and will obtain other glimpses hereafter, I will now compliment the first of the above opinions by taking a rapid glance over the surface of Southern society, and see if we can discover any social element there of a nature to justify such a belief.

Southern Society.

It is in Northern society that the democratic principles most manifest their license; because its laboring population, constituting a majority of the inhabitants, and as a class no better than the same class in all countries, are raised by the democratic principles to a political importance which enables them at any time, by their votes, to determine elections and influence the policy of government. It is in such communities that the dogmas of liberty of conscience, popular sovereignty, and universal equality tell with fatal effect.

In Southern society, on the contrary, these principles are comparatively harmless; because their excesses are counteracted to no small degree by the system of labor established there. The basis of labor being negro slavery, the country is restricted to a comparatively choice population of whites. Four millions of slaves, (numerically equal almost to the whites,) who are denied the elective franchise, go a long way to neutralize the ruinous effects of universal suffrage, and to limit the absolute quality of popular sovereignty. Liberty of conscience, free inquiry, and endless discussion find, to some extent, a counterpoise in the same arrangement. Above all, the dogma of equality, while it is limited in its effects, is also practically refuted, by a large population of efficient laborers, who daily manifest their moral and intellectual inferiority by their servility, and by a thousand evidences of incapacity for any other position in civilized life than the one they occupy. In short, all the absolute dogmas of democracy lose much of their energy and virulence when brought in contact with this single element of Southern society.

From the system of slavery proceed nearly all the other social conditions of the South: it is a nucleus around which all her social relations precipitate themselves, and form a homogeneous society of which domestic slavery is the central principle. In consequence of this arrangement, the populations of the South are almost exclusively rural: with few exceptions, her very towns possess more of a sylvan than an urban character: agriculture, which separates the laborers in small squads at vast intervals apart, is the main employment of the country; and the strict discipline which is observed renders large reunions both difficult and innoxious. Under such conditions, dangerous disturbances are not only of rare occurrence, but it is next to impossible for them to happen at all. The perfect subordination of the laborers, spread thinly over wide surfaces: the isolation of families, forming diminutive centers of small communities bound together by the closest ties of mutual affection, dependence, and interest: the peaceful occupations of husbandry: the plenty which everywhere abounds: the almost utter absence of want: the intimate communion with nature; all things, in short, tend to tranquilize society, and exclude the excitements and riotous scenes so common in denser communities and in large manufacturing districts crowded with free white laborers, who are at the same time noisy politicians, debaters, and voters.

The intricate relations of capital and labor disturb not the social quietude of the South; for her capital and labor are united and harmonious: nor are her slumbers broken by a growing apprehension of an ever-increasing preponderance of the laboring classes: nor by the rise and progress of a pauper population. There the rights of property are never assailed, nor ever likely to be, except from abroad. No such an episode of modern civilization as Mormonism could have proceeded from the bosom of her society. Associations of "Free Lovers," "Women's Rights," "Communists," "Socialists," are never heard of in the South, except as echoes from the North.

Contrasts, reliefs, are as much needed in the moral as in the external world. No large society can do well without them. They are needed as countervailing influences, as reciprocating opposites, to draw off and counteract on the one hand the excesses of each other, and to intensify on the other the national life. As long as the equilibrium of political force was maintained between the two sections, the government worked comparatively well: the South attempted no interference with Northern institutions: there was a continual interchange of benefits: it was all give and take. I will not say, as some have said, that the South gave more than she took; though that may be possible, it is hardly probable: it is more likely the advantages were mutual, and it is certain they were incalculable. Volumes would be needed to enumerate all the material exchanges and courtesies that aggrandized and beautified the social life of the two sections, until the preponderance of political force was transferred in a large degree to the North. Then, instantly, these fine relations ceased: the *entente cordiale* was interrupted: the disturbing power of the democratic principles manifested itself: criminations and recriminations followed: aggressions and retaliations began; and human folly culminated in this monstrous crime.

It will not do to say that the democratic principles had nothing to do with this crime: that they are not responsible for the follies and vices of men; and that revolutions are liable to occur in governments where democracy never reigned. Democracy has caused every revolution which has taken place in the nations of Christendom during the last three hundred years. It cannot be denied that the democratic principles were directly responsible for the abolition fanaticism at the North: for the separation of the churches North and South: for the bloody feuds in Kansas: for the John Brown raid into Virginia: for the election of Mr. Lincoln on purely sectional and party grounds: for the higher law doctrine: for the right of individual interpretations of laws and constitutions: for the doctrine of State rights and its derivative right of peaceable secession; and that all those events were but preludes to the swelling theme of the present grand climax—the legitimate *finale* to such ominous preparations.

So far was Southern society from possessing any disturbing quality, of which the North had a right to complain, that the society itself, in view of the disorganizing tendencies at the North, was a saving clause in the constitution of the general society of the country from which the North, at some future day, might have derived immense advantage. If a perfect balance of power could have been maintained between the two sections, not only would those material exchanges described above have been kept up, and the national character have been decorated and beautified by many courtesies and amenities of social life, but the conservative quality of Southern society would have gone far to have staved off to an indefinite period the peril now so imminent to Northern communities.

Reconstruction of the Union.

But peace and those thousand benefits, ornamental and useful, having passed away with the transferrence of power, it now remains to consider whether and how peaceable relations can be restored, and whether and how a reconstruction of the Union can be effected: or in the event of a final separation, what are likely to be the probable effects of the war, and the consequent dissolution of the Union, upon the respective destinies of the two nations.

This is a question of immense magnitude, and surrounded with many supreme difficulties. In the present attitude of affairs, there would seem to be no way open to a restoration of peace; and as for a reconstruction of the Union, that event appears to be as far removed from human understandings, or a probability of achievement, as the squaring of the circle. There are many excellent persons in the South whose patriotism will be shocked by the bare statement of such a proposition as the restoration of the Union. In their opinion, the bloody fields, broken hearts, ruined fortunes of the South cry aloud for vengeance on the ruthless invader: until these be atoned, and a fit retribution be visited on the latter, their wrath, like that of Achilles, will know no abatement.

There is no question but that vengeance will be meted out to all parties according to their deserts; for the moral government of this world is too well adjusted for offenses to pass unpunished. Who are the guilty, who the innocent, are not questions for us, with our passions and prejudices, to determine. Then let us leave vengeance to whom it properly belongs, and think no more of it.

Time and the unfolding of events will no doubt solve this momentous problem in their own unprecedented way; but also wise men, who will think without heat and act without passion, can greatly facilitate the decision, and at the same time obviate unnumbered woes which will arise if the solution be left to the blind forces of nature, or to the natural course of events. It is not to be supposed that the destiny of this great country is abandoned to the mere *hazards* of war: much less is it consigned to the follies or caprices of a few silly individuals; *chance* has as little to do with the fate of this nation as with the creation of the world: the course of its civilization is predetermined by the laws of Infinite Reason, which man cannot contravene; and however its progress may be retarded or harassed by his crimes and imbecilities, the eternal fitness and relation of things will still carry it forward to its prescribed end. But

Providence is not wise for the sake of absolving men from their duty. God has endowed us with reason in order that we might help him to direct our own affairs in a rational and not in a blind manner. In the providential government of the world there is ample room left for the exercise of human virtue and folly, for the devotion of the hero and the selfishness of the coward. What, therefore, we can neither prevent nor accomplish, we can at least delay or hasten by our good or bad conduct.

If there be any analogy in human affairs, or in the epochs of history, we might possibly derive some light from the past of humanity, or at least some consolation in our misery by a comparison with other nations and ages. One of the main obstacles in the way of a settlement seems to be the novelty of our environments: not that the situation is unprecedented in history, but that it is new to us, we never having had any such experience before. As a people, taken *en masse*, we know little of, and care less for, the social crises of past times. And yet those times, if we interrogate them, might direct us the route to our true destination. So far from being a historical novelty, our situation is the commonest event of the ages and the nations. During anterior epochs, scarcely a generation of mankind has been allowed to pass off the stage of life without participating in, or witnessing, an internecine war such as ours. The blood that has been spilt, the hearts that have been broken, the fortunes ruined, the resentments roused, have not been less than our own: in many cases, far greater; and yet they seem to have been no bar to reconciliations. Witness the civil wars of England; and witness too her perfect national unity at this day.

During the course of the sixteenth century, the emancipation of the human mind in spiritual matters, and the centralization of power in temporal affairs, triumphed at one and the same time all over Europe. The first was a victory over the absolute power of the Church; the second established itself on the ruins of feudalism. So far, liberty of conscience and absolute monarchy were in close alliance: they marched abreast over the ramparts of the ancient ecclesiastical order and the ancient feudal and municipal liberty. No sooner was this double triumph achieved, than the struggle between monarchy and democracy in civil society began. The first shock between these two forces took place in England. If we except the wars of the Roses, which were more dynastic than reformative, all the civil wars of England, posterior to that epoch, were wars of liberty against despotism; but it was the liberty of the people against the despotism of the crown; the liberty of the many against the tyranny of one. The crown had too many prerogatives, the people too few. Royalty proclaimed itself absolute and superior to all laws; the people claimed their ancient prerogatives. Issue was joined upon these points, and the trial was by battle. A series of revolutions followed. Each revolution was a step toward an equilibrium of the political forces so unequally divided: from each revolution, the people came out with a little more power, and the king with a little less; until finally, after more than a hundred years of conflicts and truces, a perfect balance of power was obtained, and peace settled down permanently upon the nation.

Such was the real nature of the struggle which began

in England about the year of grace 1640. But the nation was very far from understanding the exact nature of the case, as I have described it. She knew not distinctly what she required, or what she was in search of. She had not the slightest conception of the immense magnitude of the quarrel, of the true points at issue, or of the stupendous results to which it was to lead. So far as her knowledge of the grand ends to be obtained was concerned, she was a blind instrument in the hands of a superior power. The first thing that strikes us in that famous history is the apparent insignificance of the origin of those celebrated wars, the low aims and mean purposes for which they were begun. The great English Rebellion, as it was called, was brought about ostensibly by an attempt of the king to collect a tax of twenty shillings of ship money, which one John Hampden, a gentleman of large fortune, refused to pay. But this slight cause was only the exterior envelope of ends incomparably greater. Those sublime ends, of which no one thought at the time, of which no one was conscious, were attained after many long years of hard fighting. The others, the base motives, the wretched personalities, the individual passions engaged in the strife, and which alone preoccupied the minds of all the actors,—they, after making for a moment so much noise in the world, sink into deep oblivion, and degenerate into uncertain anecdotes, which ordinary history may search for and collect, but which the philosophy of history neglects as indifferent to humanity.

In the war now raging in this country, the parties litigant are reversed; the actors have changed sides: the cause is the same; the ends are the same. It is still liberty, security, an equilibrium of political power which is required, and which is sought for, though no one seems to know it. But, in this case, it is the people who are the despots: the people have too much power, the government too little. It is the tyranny of the many which now oppresses society. The people have proclaimed themselves absolute, and superior to all laws and constitutions. The minority have no guarantees of security against the majority. It is to achieve liberty against license, order against anarchy, that this war is waged. It is to restore an equilibrium of political forces; to re-establish the lost balance of power; to check the excesses of one set of principles by the introduction of a countervailing set; to take the government from party and restore it to humanity, to the nation; to obtain guarantees for the execution of laws and the observance of the constitution,—these are the purposes, the supreme objects of this revolution. It is the rebellion of Society against the People; of the people against themselves. It is the cause of Civilization which is being tried. It is the Future *versus* the Present which is the style of the suit. These great ends cannot but be accomplished, though it may require a hundred years for their achievement; for society cannot rest until based on their firm foundation. The other motives, the paltry ambitions, the trivial interests, the fanaticisms, the hatreds, the prejudices, the spirit of revenge, whatever, in short, is personal or individual, however they may figure in the strife, will disappear from the grand *denouement* of the drama, and live, if at all, only in memoirs and biographies.

In view of these facts, of the clear purposes manifested by present hostilities, of the social wants of the nation, of the known ends to be obtained, is it too much to expect that rational men will hasten to anticipate the designs of the Revolution, and terminate the war by granting all its demands? How this is to be done, good men and true only can determine. Let there be a grand inquest of the nation: let Virtue and Wisdom preside over it; and the issue cannot be doubtful.

But if this be not done, and the war be allowed to terminate the quarrel in its own way: what, in that case, is likely to happen? In that case, one of two things is very likely to happen: either the Southern Confederacy will gain its independence, or it will not.

The Consequences of Southern Independence.

We will consider the first of these alternatives, as it was the avowed object of the war, and suppose the independence of the Southern Confederacy achieved, and the process of decomposition begun by a separation of the Northern and Southern States. Is there any guarantee that this division, which will be the first, shall be the last? What is to arrest the further continuance of the process, and save society from dissolution? The doctrine of State rights has met with the most signal success: it has established its rule by conquest: it has won its spurs on the field of battle: it has demolished all opposition: it has no rival in the field of politics: the worst derivative of democracy, it will have accomplished not only itself, but it will have established also its own darling derivative, the right of secession: flushed with victory, then, what is to stay its progress? Is there anything in the new constitution calculated to protect the Confederate States from endless subdivisions? Is the new alliance more binding than the old? Has the Southern league, by reason of some secret virtue which is in it, so limited the democratic dogmas that they shall be constrained to act with modest forbearance, and insure order without tyranny and progress without excesses? Is society any better protected from the caprices of opinion than before? In short, has the Southern Confederacy constructed a political system which, in the whole of its active development, shall be always fully consequent on its own principles, and furnish accordant solutions on all the various leading questions of the national polity? If this be not so, then whither are we drifting?

It is certain we are not tending toward order and security: for those social virtues we shall be solely dependent, as heretofore, upon the reserve of popular good sense, or be indebted for them to the intellectual inertia so common to masses of men. But how long can that generous forbearance, or that mental sluggishness, be counted on to endure? How long shall the doctrine of State rights, so confident of its approved strength, be able to suppress its disorganizing instincts? The answer is patent: until a day or an hour furnish a provocation or a temptation. Then, perhaps, will recur another series of bloody fields, broken hearts, ruined fortunes. And this miserable routine will be kept up, until American society shall perish in its own decompositions, and American civilization be consigned to the receptacle of things lost on the earth, provided God, in his displeasure, should conclude to abandon us to our follies.

We know the tendency of everything is to excess: hence the necessity for checks and guards. If State sovereignty, in the paroxysm of another freak, see proper to reassert its claim, shall the Confederate States ignore its own principles, deny its own arguments, and refuse the contumacious State or States the right of peaceable secession? If so, whence will it derive its authority? If not, what will bind together the States? The interests of the States are by no means identical. The pursuits of many of them are different, and will call for corresponding differences of legislation. In short, there are diversities, however slight in appearances, sufficient to create antagonistic views on many social questions of the first importance. These antagonisms will find their simplest and easiest solution in secession, where that doctrine is the recognized policy of the nation, and the voluntary obedience of the States is their only co-ordinating principle.

These views and questions are not wholly hypothetical: they are founded upon the nature of the Confederacy itself; and the consequences they suggest must flow necessarily from the establishment of such a system. But, in order to verify this assertion, I will now examine a little nearer into the real nature, meaning, and intent of this Confederation of States, and into other consequences likely to flow from its actual character and purposes, as gathered from the design of the framers of it. In order, then, to arrive at a correct understanding of the true nature of the present arrangement, we must examine it by the light with which Mr. Calhoun has furnished us: we must construe it by his interpretation of the composition of the old United

States: we must apply to it the pet phrases by which that gentleman attempted to fritter away the binding force of the Federal constitution; and in which design, as things have turned out, he was but too successful. These pet phrases of Mr. Calhoun were "constitutional compact," as being more accurately descriptive of the real character of the Federal constitution than any other phrase; and also the word "accede," as descriptive of the manner by which the States entered the old Union. These phrases, of course, were designed to cover a *pet* idea of that gentleman, which, interpreted, means this: That the several States formed a "constitutional *compact,*" not a union, to which each State *acceded* as a separate sovereign community: that its sovereignty was not lost, or in least impaired, by this *accession:* that the States delegated to the General government certain specified powers, to be exercised jointly, reserving, at the same time, each State to itself the residuary mass of powers, to be exercised by its own separate government: that the General government was not made the final judge of the powers delegated to it: that it had no right to pass judgment on the constitutionality of congressional laws; but that this right belonged to the States: that, as in all cases of compact among sovereign parties, without any common judge, each party has an equal right to judge for itself, as well of the infraction of the compact as of the mode and measure of redress.

According to Mr. Calhoun's political confession of faith, it was further declared: that the people of the United States never were *united* on the principle of the social compact: that they were never formed into *one nation* or *people:* that the States composing the Union always retained their sovereignty: that the allegiance of their citizens was never transferred to the General government: that, in point of fact, the people of the United States never did owe allegiance to the government of the United States; and that the States themselves never did part with the right of punishing treason, or with any other right of sovereignty.

In using the phrase *constitutional* compact, the object of Mr. Calhoun was to make the *name* of the government accord with the above idea of it. But, in reality, the word *constitutional,* in this connection, conveys no definite idea whatever: because a "*compact*" is identical with league, treaty, convention; they are all synonyms, alternative words, and cover the same meaning, describe the same thing, or at least things between which there is no essential difference; and when those words are employed to describe the acts of sovereign States, we would find it difficult to understand what was meant by a "*constitutional* league or treaty between England and France, or a *constitutional* convention between Austria and Russia." With equal propriety, we might speak of a "*constitutional* indenture of copartnership, a *constitutional* deed of conveyance, or a *constitutional* bill of exchange."

As to the other term of Mr. Calhoun's phraseology, descriptive of the manner by which the States entered the old Union, that, too, was not without its peculiar significance. The converse of the phrase "*accede*" is *secede:* so that *accession* implies *secession;* and the right to *accede* carries with it the right to *secede.* The meaning of the word *accede,* when applied to political associations, is to become a party, by agreeing to the terms of a treaty, by one hitherto a stranger to it, as the *accession* of a king to a confederacy. In this connection, the word *accede* implies an act of sovereignty, and carries the same implication to its converse *secede*. Whether or not this phrase was correctly used by Mr. Calhoun, admits of doubt. At least, the propriety of its employment, in the case to which he applied it, was disputed, and, if not refuted, was ably discussed by Mr. Webster. The propriety of its application, however, to the present Confederacy admits of no doubt, and renders *secession* an indisputable right appertaining to the *acceding* parties; so far at least as mere verbal authority, or the rules of syntax, can confer that right.

Such, then, according to Mr. Calhoun's political evangel, was the composition of the old United States, and such the nature of the old Federal constitution. Whether or not this be the true gospel, in the respect of the old association, I pretend not to decide here. In any case, whether true or false in *theory*, it has been terribly true in *practice*. It will be perceived that this interpretation renders the several States as absolutely sovereign and independent as ever were the ancient Greek Republics, or the modern Italian States; and that, according to such a construction, it would be as impossible to bind them steadfastly in one united empire, or to give to them a radical unity, as it was to unite its ancient Greek or modern Italian political congeners. The public acts, therefore, of a national government formed upon such a basis must necessarily be, to all intents and purposes, in the last resort and in the last analysis of no manner of effect whatever. Because, it is clear if the States should ever exercise their sovereign right of secession, which they can do at any moment with or without cause alleged, there would then be no power left to execute treaties, pay debts, or fulfill any other obligation. And furthermore, if the General government should declare war, one State, exercising her sovereign right, might, if she saw proper to do so, make peace for herself: or if the General government should make peace, one State might continue the war on her own account. In such event, the General government, or the other States, would have no other means of redress, except by waging war on the contumacious State; but that would be equivalent to a dissolution of the Confederacy.

Now, this was precisely the nature of the *compact* which existed between the States, under the old Articles of Confederation, anterior to the adoption of the late Federal constitution. Under that Confederation, Congress issued its requisitions on the States for their quota of money for national purposes, and the States neglected them: there was no power of coercion but war; and Mr. Jefferson, in 1786–87, actually recommended this remedy to be tried. "There will be no money in the treasury," said he, "till the Confederacy shows its teeth;" and he suggested that a single frigate would soon levy, on the commerce of the delinquent State, the deficiency of its contribution. But this, again, would be war; and it is evident, as Mr. Webster said, that a Confederacy could not long hold together which should be at war with its members. The present Southern Confederacy bears a very close resemblance, in many respects, to the old Confederation of the States; and as such, it is a retrogression of nearly a century to a wretched condition of things from which the States escaped with great difficulty and trouble.

A confederacy, then, is identical with a compact, a league, a convention. And a confederacy of sovereign communities, such as exists in the South, is nothing else but a subsisting or continuing *treaty*, which rests for support solely on the plighted faith of the sovereign party. This, indeed, is substantially the definition which Mr. Webster gives of a confederacy; and if his authority be not good, there is none better in the world. The Southern Confederacy, therefore, has no inherent power of its own to enforce a fulfillment or continuance of the treaty, longer than each of the States may see proper voluntarily to observe it. As sovereigns, the States are subject to no superior power: each must judge for itself of any alleged violation of the compact; and if such violation be supposed to have occurred, each may adopt any mode or measure of redress which it shall think proper to employ. Such is the nature of a treaty, that "if a league between sovereign powers have no limitation as to the time of its duration, and contain nothing making it perpetual, it subsists only during the good pleasure of the parties, although no violation be complained of." Nay, even though the confederation or treaty be declared, by one of its stipulations, to be perpetual, still it is evident that it subsists only during the good pleasure of either of the sovereign parties, although no violation be complained of. It was on this principle that "the Congress of the United States, in 1798, declared null and void the treaty of alliance between the United States and France, though it professed to be a perpetual alliance."

If a violation of the terms of the confederacy be alleged, and the injuries be serious, or only pretended, the suffering party, being sovereign and sole judge of its own mode and method of redress, may indemnify itself by reprisals; by cruising against the property of the other members of the league; by authorizing captures, and making open war. If, then, it be well understood that such is the nature of the Southern Confederacy, and with past experience of the instability of such governments or leagues, how is it conceivable that the Confederacy could even hope to obtain respect and credit abroad? What foreign power would enter into treaty with it? Who would lend it money? What guarantees could it give for the fulfillment of public treaties, for the payment of public debts, or for the continuance of its own existence during a day or an hour? Such a government, now that we know its antecedents, would be unable to inspire the least sense of security; prudent citizens would not invest their means in real estate lying within its limits; foreign capital would shun it, and domestic capital would flow out of it. In short, it is difficult to conceive how such a confederacy could hold together during one generation, or even one decade.

In Church governments, where the only territory over which the exercise of authority is to be extended is the conscience, there any species of force is no doubt unwise, impolitic, and illegitimate, for convictions cannot be coerced; in such case, voluntary obedience is the only rule of action. Or, if the assumptions of democracy were true; if all men were equal, equally wise and just, and their wisdom and justice were supreme and infallible, then compulsion would not be needed, nor would even government itself be needed. But as long as human nature remains as it is, civil government will always be obliged to employ force to make itself obeyed. There is no way of avoiding this; it is a necessary consequence of human imperfection—an imperfection which resides as well in power as in society, in nations as in individuals. Then, in the absence of any method of coercion, to suppose that a large number of States, with jealous ideas of sovereignty, scattered over a vast extent of territory, with greater or less diversity of interests, will remain confederated together for any considerable length of time, and yield a voluntary obedience to all the laws which democracy, in its spirit of excessive legislation, shall see proper to enact, is a dream as wild as was ever hatched in the brain of insanity. If there be no organized force within sufficient for that purpose, an external pressure, such as neighboring hostile States, might serve to bind the States together for awhile; but that is a very doubtful principle of cohesion, and wholly unreliable. Under existing circumstances, therefore, a dissolution of the Confederacy, at no distant day, would seem to be inevitable; and whatever consequences, good or bad, are liable to result from such a state of social decomposition, are as certain to take place as if they were already an accomplished fact. That these consequences cannot be good, no arguments are needed to prove; that they will be fraught with dire evils to humanity and civilization, follows as a matter of course.

But if, owing to the conservative element of slavery left in Southern society, a greater degree of permanence be secured to social order and a co-ordination of the States there, how will the case stand with the Northern tier of States? As soon as the integrity of the Union shall have been violated by the contemplated division, the contagion will have begun, the force of example will be strong, new interests will solicit new combinations, and the passions and follies of men, under the noxious inspiration of the democratic principles, will again be too strong for the dictates of reason and common sense. Under these conditions, the social affinities remaining in the North would scarcely be sufficient to overcome the various antagonisms and disorganizing influences which would be forever repelling the States from each other. At first, the States would no doubt slough off in sections. The Northwestern States could easily imagine that they have few interests in common with the New England States; and there are many hostile influences which would tend to detach them from each other. The Pacific States are too far off to derive much benefit from an adhesion to any portion of the old Union which might hang together; and, in their case, there are geographical divisions, and many natural causes, which might suggest the propriety of a separate national independence. In the end, in all probability, only alliances offensive and defensive would be entered into by the States, as between foreign nations; and the drama of the little Greek Republics of antiquity, with its melancholy catastrophe, would be re-enacted here on a somewhat enlarged theater. If the parts of Appelles, Demosthenes, Pericles, and other divine masters of Grecian Art, Eloquence, and War, could be reproduced also, the evil would not be wholly uncompensated.

Now, I do not pretend to say that the recurrence of such a state of things is even possible, much less probable: because the nature of modern civilization happily forbids it; and the nature of modern civilization, with equal felicity, forbids also the first division, or any division whatever. I am only pointing out the tendency of the ideas engaged in this movement,—ideas which seem to rule the Southern mind wholly as to its social plans for the future, and of whose tendencies, or of the impossibility of their practical achievement, it appears to be as ignorant as if it were set three thousand years back, at the commencement of History, with no Past to enlighten it. In order to expose more fully yet the deceptive character of those ideas, and discover whither we are drifting, if Providence should abandon us to our own guidance, I will continue the perspective a little further.

Assuming, then, that the integrity of each of the two Republics will be preserved, that the unity of each will remain unbroken, and no further decompositions take place after the first division: how, in that case, are their international relations to be regulated? Will hostilities cease suddenly and forever with the subsidence of present disturbances? Will each nation be permitted to actualize in peace its own social ideas, and to develop undisturbed a civilization that shall contradict the idiosyncrasies or shock the sensibilities of the other? Will that great element of modern civilization, commerce, by its rivalries, its wondrous activity, its myriad individual interests, throw no obstacles in the way of peaceable relations? There are no natural divisions—no British Channel, no Alps, no Pyrenees, no Mediterranean, Baltic, or Black Seas, no Chersonese, no Bosphorus, no Greek and Italian Peninsulas, or, in their absence, no

Chinese Wall or other artificial barrier sufficient to localize the two nations and protect them from each other. Everywhere, on the proposed line of division, they touch, and, in a manner, surround each other. Everywhere the country is open to invasion, and invites aggression. In many places the two frontiers run into each other and interlock, as if protesting, by their friendly embrace, against the political separation of that which God hath joined together. The same protest is made, with still more emphasis, by the Mississippi River: that stream binds the Mississippi Valley indissolubly, as if with bands of iron and brass; while it flows to the Gulf of Mexico, it will bear upon its bosom the tide of war, and its waves will redden with the blood of hostile armies, unless the geographical unity of its great valley unite into one nation the peoples who inhabit its upper and lower shores. And, finally, the customs' regulations, along an almost boundless inland frontier, thus interlaced, will not diminish the chances of collision: nor will those social parasites, the demagogues, simplify relations already too complex for international tranquillity.

If the institution of slavery, the immediate occasion of the war and the separation, was deemed insecure in the old Union, when the government of a mighty nation and a thousand material interests were pledged to its protection, what will be its condition when those guards, feeble as they may have been considered, are withdrawn from around it? Will our slaves escape less into the free States, now become a foreign, perhaps a hostile, nation? or will the Federal Congress pass other fugitive slave laws for their restitution?

These are all questions which can arise only after the accomplishment of a revolution. While the Union lasts, they do not disturb us; they are then no questions at all; they spring up to startle and haunt us only from its grave. They are the dragon's teeth which we have sown; and if we succeed in our design, they will make the land bristle with bayonets, and yield us only the bloody harvests of war and death.

Secession.

The above notice of the slavery question in this connection leads us to a review of the conduct of the Southern people in their adoption of secession as a remedy for their real or fancied wrongs. A very slight examination will suffice to show how far they were or were not justified in the employment of a measure which has turned out to be so disastrous, and which, instead of curing, has magnified the evil, and made that which was bad enough before a thousand times worse. The same examination will disclose, too, to what extent the principles of democracy have contributed, by their demoralization of the mind of Southern society, to the precipitation of the present crisis.

Whatever else may be said of it, the Federal constitution was at least not inimical to Southern interests: on the contrary, it did all it could do to protect the rights of the slave States. If some of the Northern States, by factious legislation, violated in *effect* one of its solemn provisions, which was of peculiar interest to the South, it was no fault of the constitution; and the Federal government, up to the day and hour of secession, was innocent of any bad faith on the slavery question. To the best of its abilities, it had always guarded the rights of property in the South as well as in the North; and those clauses of the constitution which referred directly to the subject of slavery were perhaps the only important ones which had entirely escaped the impingement of executive aggression. While, on all other questions of moment, the General government had been accused of attempts to trespass upon the constitution, and to stretch its authority beyond the warrant of that instrument, not the slightest imputation of Punic faith had ever attached to it on the subject of slavery. Amid the storms raised by the abolitionists, the Federal government, whether the President came from the North or South, had ever stood as firm as a rock. Against that indomitable barrier the waves of fanaticism had always broken themselves to pieces, and lay quelled at its base. When fanaticism, thus rebuked, turned its attention to the States, and was seducing some of them into its embraces, Congress, at the solicitation of the South, hastened to pass all the laws the latter required to strengthen the constitution and protect slavery. It was so well understood by the earnest abolitionists that the Federal constitution and Federal government were the only lions in their path, that they deemed their removal a prerequisite of success, and advocated a dissolution of the Union for that express purpose. By an infatuation which would almost seem to have been the work of the gods, the South rushed upon its destiny, and did that for its enemies which they could scarcely have ever done for themselves at all. Those abolitionists, therefore, who understand their business and the means best adapted to their trade, rejoice at this madness of the South, and hail secession as a sure earnest of success. They make no disguise of their satisfaction, and are as much opposed to reconstruction, until their abolition work is accomplished, as the South itself can be.

In no correct sense could the election of Mr. Lincoln have been regarded as a triumph of abolitionism proper. He was himself no abolitionist: he was a free-soiler only. The abolitionists could not have elected a candidate of their own: they therefore did the next best thing in their power—they coalesced with the free-soilers; and by their alliance did that for the free-soil candidate which the free-soil party could not have done by itself. However strong may be the affinity between the two political sects, the Abolitionists and Republicans, they are so far from being identical in sentiments or measures that many extreme abolitionists refused to cast their votes for Mr. Lincoln, and to this day withhold their confidence from him.

In the absence of any positive information on that subject, it would be sheer folly to speculate as to what might have been the policy or the general tendency of Mr. Lincoln's administration, if the South, hurried on by an excited imagination, anticipating what of evil it knew not, and prejudging Mr. Lincoln's course, had not, by its premature action, forced him, perhaps against his wishes, wholly into the arms of the abolitionists. If any faith is to be attached to Mr. Lincoln's own declarations, and to the plain wording of the platform on which he was elected, nothing is left to conjecture on that subject. But secession, it seems, like Satan reproving sin, refuses to believe anything abolitionism can say, when the latter denies its evil intentions.

Rejecting, then, all such disclaimers on the part of Lincoln and the abolitionists as wholly unreliable, when weighed against the passions of fanaticism, and reasoning solely from presumptive evidence, we are still forced, from whatever point of view we may look at it, into conclusions adverse to the policy of secession. That measure, whether regarded as a means of defense against real or supposed injuries, or as the expression of an abstract political principle, is equally indefensible. On purely moral grounds, it is still more reprehensible. Like abolitionism, it is a species of political fanaticism, thrown off by the disorganizing tendencies of the democratic principles; and as such it was bound to have its day of grace, to reach its point of culmination, to commit its *maximum* of evil, and then sink in darkness forever.

But to resume our line of argument. It is hardly conceivable that, with the plain letter of the constitution before him, and his solemn oath to support it, Mr. Lincoln could have been so far recreant to the obligations of honor and duty as to have committed a double crime in a single act by violating the one at the expense of the other; for a violation of the constitution would have been a violation of his oath, a sacrifice of both duty and honor at one and the same time. And thus to treason he would have added perjury for no other conceivable reason than to subserve the nefarious ends of a reckless party, in whose prejudices he did not participate, and of whose fanaticism he did not partake. They who believe oaths and duties are so easily violated, must themselves have very loose notions of such obligations, and judge others from their own consciences.

It is no answer to this argument to point to Mr. Lincoln's alleged unconstitutional acts since his inauguration. In the first place, for those acts, if they be unconstitutional, it is well known he shelters himself under the plea of "military necessity,"—a plea which, in cases of flagrant war, is recognized as being well laid: in any case, whether right or wrong, it is a plea for which secession itself is directly responsible, for it alone furnished him with it. In the second place, it is not at all probable that, but for the previous action of the South anticipating his administration, and perhaps wrongly prejudging it, he would have so completely surrendered himself to the guidance of the abolitionists, whose active support he deemed himself forced, by the necessities of his situation, to procure at any price. True, if this motive be well charged against him, his conduct is indefensible upon any such ground: none but a weak-minded man, in a case of that kind, where his duty lay plain before him, would have ignored its dictates, and swerved from the path of rectitude, under the plea of necessity. Wisdom and virtue combined would have decided very differently; and the country has the right to look for this combination in one who is the elect, the choicest mind, of a great nation of thirty millions of population.

Evil never does anything right. There can be no doubt that Mr. Lincoln's administration, since its unreserved surrender to abolitionism, has been a most vicious one, and its policy the very worst that could have been adopted: of all other policies, it was the one least capable of bringing the war to a speedy and happy termination; and the one best adapted to prolong it to the latest period. No other line of conduct was so well qualified to deepen the malignity of the strife, to cause the greatest amount of slaughter, to bring about so much unnecessary individual suffering and ruin without any compensating advantage, to plant in the hearts of men those bitter hatreds, that spirit of revenge, which, for the time being, transfer hell to earth, convert men into fiends, and render reconciliation that much more difficult and distant.

But, notwithstanding all this, secession is not the proper party to bring accusations against abolitionism on the score of unconstitutionality or any other vice: its own huge crimes disqualify it from becoming a public accuser: before it can consistently arraign the sins of others, it must purge itself of its own darker ones. Abolitionism and secession must, both of them, be considered in no other light than as two evil principles in conflict, for which the democratic principles are directly responsible; and it is devoutly to be hoped they will end the strife by mutually destroying each other, when honesty may stand some chance to come by its own. It is not to justify the crimes of one of these principles by enumerating the faults of the other that this book is written, but to demonstrate how wantonly wicked both of them are, and yet how inevitable they were as logical sequences of the fundamental principles of government. As secession is now under review, my object is to show that, so far from having a legitimate origin, it was justified neither by facts, nor by any presumptive evidence, nor by any sound method of hypothetical reasoning: that it was called into action by no urgent necessity: that no immediate or even an early prospective danger threatened the interest it rushed to protect; but that it hurled the country into war gratuitously, or from mistaken views, or from any motives save those which were good and true.

There is a wide difference between a party out of office, and the same party in office. It is seldom that the extreme measures advocated by an opposition are carried into practice when the responsibility which attaches to power is thrown upon its leaders. The abstract sentiment of abolitionism has long ago been converted by the demagogues into a mere political cry, an electioneering watchword, with no other meaning than belongs to all such shibboleths of party. However a few misguided fanatics may still cling to its moral sense, its original purpose, the demagogues use it only as a hobby on which to ride into power. Once there, the ambition of such persons is generally gratified; and their only after-care is to sustain themselves in their seats. To this end, they suddenly become very conservative, in order to deprecate as much as possible the violence of opposition, and because they must consider well the practicability of measures for which they are directly responsible, and which, unless they be eminently just and feasible, may work their own downfall. Men in power, in a government like this, soon learn the necessity of moderation and justice. A very short time, under the pressure of official responsibility, may have sufficed to tone down the vehemence of abolition frenzy into an eminently conservative administration. In all probability, office would have been the grave of abolitionism; and its influence, as a disturbing element of politics, might have ceased with its accession to power, if a fair and peaceable trial had been granted it, or if its passions had not been roused by the embarrassments of a terrible war like this.

But this is arguing without the record, and wide of the mark. The actual case is much stronger. The simple facts are shortly these: 1st. The platform on which Mr. Lincoln was elected recognized the constitutionality of slavery, and denied any intention of interfering with it in States where it already existed. 2d. Mr. Lincoln, though elected by the aid of the abolition vote, was himself no Abolitionist. 3d. If Southern members had kept their seats, the Abolitionists would have been so far in the minority in Congress that they would have been unable, even if they had desired, to do the least harm to slavery. 4th. During the last session of the 36th Congress, held under the administration of Mr. Buchanan, Southern members were repeatedly urged to accept constitutional amendments, by two-thirds votes of both Houses, which would secure slavery against the possibility of future disturbance, except by revolution. These generous concessions were refused by the Southern delegation.

The first and second of the above statements require no further comment; the third and fourth call for some additional notice and elucidation by proof. To the third it was objected, that the abolition party had grown so rapidly that, from an insignificant faction a few years ago, it had already expanded into the controlling power of the government; that this increase of strength was daily progressing; that it was fast absorbing the whole North; that there was no real sympathy in the breast of any man north of Mason and Dixon's line in favor of slavery or the South; that there was an innate hostility between the two sections which was inextinguishable; that very soon abolitionism would be in a position to dictate its ideas to the nation; that it would be madness for the South to wait until the enemy was in actual possession of the government; that the property of the South would be ultimately confiscated by it, unless the former sought timely safety in secession, which was the only protection she had for her rights against the slow but sure abrasions of abolition aggression.

To these objections all I have to say is, they were not verified by facts. At the time they were made, abolitionism was *not* the controlling power of the government: if it has become so since, temporarily and for a special purpose, it is because secession made it so. So far from increasing with such rapidity as to threaten an early absorption of the entire North, it is now matter of history that at the first congressional election, after Mr. Lincoln's inauguration, the Abolitionists were defeated in every Northern State in which elections were held. If the tide of Northern votes has since turned in favor of the government, it is because the stubborn resistance of the South has made it necessary to the integrity of the Union, and to the very existence of the North itself, to suppress the rebellion at any price. But it is the propriety and necessity of secession as a remedial measure at the time of its adoption which I am now discussing, and not the propriety or necessity of the means employed by the Federal government, and sanctioned by the North, for its suppression.

I now approach the fourth and last of the above statements; and in order to show the Southern people who were their real enemies, and who the authors of their present ruin, I propose to place this controversy in a light still more clear, and to answer all hypothetical objections by *facts* which are of record and not to be disputed or argued about. For this purpose I shall run over the journals of the last session of Congress held under Mr. Buchanan's administration, and extract from them everything relating to this matter. The review will disclose to the Southern people how effectually they allowed themselves to be deluded by their treacherous servants. Whether the delusion were willingly or unwillingly embraced; whether the people were deceived because they wished to be deceived; and whether, if they had been all the time well advised of what was going on, they would or would not have supported their representatives in the course they pursued, are questions for themselves to answer to their own consciences. I shall acquit my duty by revealing some of the secrets of that important session of Congress, which, to my certain knowledge, were known to very few persons in the South at the time of their occurrence. The Southern press, to its eternal disgrace, partook of the treason of her congressional demagogues, and was silent then, when, of all times, it ought to have been most faithfully communicative.

The last session of the 36th Congress assembled on the 3d day of December, 1860. During that session, or rather on that day, the Senate was composed of twenty-five Abolition and Republican members on one side, and thirty-five Southern and Northern conservative members on the other side. The Abolitionists and Republicans were so far from being identical, that I shall not designate them by one name, nor class them as one party. Indeed, so far from voting together on all questions touching Southern interests, it will be seen that the Republicans generally voted against their Abolition allies. The Southern and Northern conservative members, on the contrary, were, on all such questions, a unit. The Northern Democrats uniformly voted with the South on all matters touching her interests, and were prepared to go almost any lengths to meet her wishes.

It will be seen, then, by this classification, that the South had, on her side, a clear majority of ten in the Senate; and if the Republicans who voted with her on many important questions be counted, the majority was much greater, sufficiently great indeed to have carried by a two-thirds vote any amendment of the constitution which the South might have desired for the better security of slavery. In the House of Representatives her majority was proportionately quite as large; and there, too, the same phenomenon on the part of the Republicans was repeated. To say, therefore, that the South, during this session of Congress, was unable to procure the passage of any law, or compromise, or concession, or amendment of the constitution she might have asked for, is simply preposterous. It will be seen, as we advance, that the only difficulty was to get her representatives to accept of any such measures, even when, in the friendly spirit of compromise, they were good-naturedly thrust upon them in spite of all their efforts to the contrary. All that Southern members had to do, as facts will prove, was to propose the measures most agreeable to them, and they would instantly have passed into laws; or, if required, they would have been engrafted, by a two-thirds vote of both Houses, into the constitution of the United States. But so far from desiring such compromises, all the efforts of Southern representatives were directed, as I shall show, to defeat every measure which was proposed for the benefit of the South. Yet such was the temper of Congress, that many resolutions, calculated to quiet the fears of the South, were offered and passed, in spite of all the treacherous schemes of Southern members to suppress them.

Such, then, was the composition, and such the conciliatory spirit of the 36th Congress, when, early in the session, Mr. Sherman, of Ohio, offered, in the House of Representatives, the following resolution, which was passed by an overwhelming majority:—

"*Resolved*, That neither Congress, nor the people, nor governments of the non-slaveholding States have the right to legislate upon or interfere with slavery in any of the slaveholding States of the Union."

On this occasion, many Republicans voted for the resolution; the Abolitionists proper all voted against it; and many Southern members refused to vote at all. The silent members offered as a plea for their contumacy, that the resolution was nothing but a law of Congress, and as such was liable to be repealed at any moment. To meet this objection, Mr. Corwin, of Ohio, an ardent Republican, proposed to engraft into the constitution, by a two-thirds vote of Congress, an amendment distinctly forbidding any Northern State or Congress from interfering, in any manner whatever, with slavery in the Southern States. This proposition was adopted, by a two-thirds vote, in the House of Representatives;

and, but for the dissolution of the Union which took place, would this day have been a part and parcel of the constitution of the United States.

On the 4th day of December, 1860, the day after Congress met, Mr. Buchanan, according to usage, delivered his Annual Message to both Houses of Congress. A large portion of his Message was devoted to what he called the distracted state of the country. Mr. Boteler, of Virginia, immediately moved that so much of the President's Message as related to the distracted state of the country be referred to a select committee of one from each State, which was agreed to. Mr. Hawkins, of Florida, as soon as his name was announced, arose and asked to be excused, saying that Florida wanted no compromise. Seven days later, Mr. Boyce, of South Carolina, asked to be excused for the same reason. Later in the session, Réuben Davis, of Mississippi, asked to be excused, because Mississippi wanted no compromise. Notwithstanding these defections, the committee proceeded to the discharge of its duties; and through Mr. Corwin, its chairman, reported the following propositions:—

1. A joint resolution to amend the constitution, by providing that no future amendment be adopted interfering with slavery in the States without the consent of all parties.

2. A bill enabling the people of New Mexico to form a constitution, and be admitted into the Union, with or without slavery.

3. A bill to amend the fugitive slave law, by removing the trial of the alleged fugitive from the jurisdiction of the State to which he had escaped, to the United

States Court of the State from which he is charged to have fled.

These resolutions were deemed to have embraced every concession the South could desire. Nothing seemed wanting to render slavery as secure as it was possible to make it. Laws had already been passed, granting to all citizens of the United States the right of removing with their property to the territories, *defining slaves to be property*, and guaranteeing protection to the owners.

The session was far advanced when the report came up for consideration. Many of the States had already seceded; and as each State left the Union, its representatives retired from Congress; comparatively few Southern members, therefore, occupied their seats when the report was called up. When first offered to the vote of the House, the report failed of receiving the requisite two-thirds majority to make it a clause of the constitution, there being 129 votes cast for it, and 70 against it. Subsequently, however, it was called up for reconsideration, and this time received the constitutional sanction of the House, having been passed by a two-thirds vote of 133 for it, to 65 against it; 48 Republicans voting for it, all the Abolitionists voting against it, and few Southern members voting at all. On the second of March, the last day but one of the session, it also passed the Senate—yeas 24, nays 12—12 Republicans voting for it, all the Abolitionists voting against it, and so many of the Southern States having seceded that there were not enough members left to act upon an amendment of the constitution to make it binding.

The bill to organize New Mexico as a State, allowing her to come into the Union with or without slavery, was laid upon the table by the contrivance of Southern members and their Northern friends—Mr. Vallandigham and his party and every Southern member then in the House voting to kill the bill by laying it on the table.

The bill to amend the fugitive slave law was passed by a vote of 92 yeas to 82 nays; 65 Republicans voting for the bill, all the Abolitionists voting against it, and very few Southern members either voting at all, or voting against it. The bill, however, failed to become a law for the want of time to consider it in the Senate.

The history of the Crittenden Compromise exhibits the same disingenuousness on the part of the representatives of the cotton States, and discloses the absurdity of attempting a reconciliation, where one party was predetermined against it on any conditions whatever. On the 3d of January, 1861, Mr. Crittenden introduced in the Senate his famous resolution, which, in substance, was nothing more than a restoration of the old Missouri Compromise line of 36° 30′, north of which slavery should be prohibited, and south of which slavery should be established. On the 14th of January, 1861, Mr. Clark, of New Hampshire, moved an amendment to Mr. Crittenden's resolution, striking out all after the word "*resolved*," and inserting, "that the provisions of the constitution, as they now are, are sufficient to maintain the unity of the Republic and the peace of the country." It was the vote to be taken on this amendment which was to decide the fate of the Compromise; and the history of this vote, and its sequel, clearly reveal the preconcerted plan and purpose of the Southern conspirators in Congress. On the nineteenth of January Clark's amendment was put to the vote. Just previous to taking the vote, a resolution to adjourn was negatived by yeas and nays—yeas 25, all Republicans and Abolitionists; nays 30, all Northern Democrats and Southern men—Mr. Douglas being unavoidably absent. This vote showed the presence of 55 Senators in the Senate Chamber, when the question, by yeas and nays, was taken on Clark's amendment, which resulted as follows: yeas 25, nays 23, being 7 votes less than on the previous vote for adjournment. The solution of this apparent anomaly is very simple: six Southern Senators sat in their seats, refusing to vote, and purposely allowing Clark's amendment to be agreed to, and the Compromise to be defeated, when they could just as easily have turned the scales the other way. The silent members were Slidell, of Louisiana; Benjamin, of Louisiana; Hemphill, of Texas; Iverson, of Georgia; Johnson, of Arkansas; Wigfall, of Texas. No sooner was the result announced to the Senate than it was flying over the wires, rousing the indignation of the Southern people with the startling intelligence that the North had refused to make any compromise, and that slavery was doomed. The consequences which were expected to follow this announcement were the immediate secession of still reluctant States; and the expectation was realized.

It would not be difficult to multiply similar evidences of treachery on the part of Southern demagogues in Congress, if indeed that can be called treachery where, for anything I know to the contrary, a majority of their constituents may have been willing victims, and would have applauded the unworthy artifices of the former if they had been known to them. But I have said enough to betray as well the *animus* of the Southern delegation as the friendly disposition toward the South of Northern members, not even excepting Republicans, the more immediate partisans of Mr. Lincoln, the President elect. It is clear, therefore, from this exposé, that when secession began there was no immediate or prospective danger threatening Southern interests, except from our own madness; and it is as certain as anything can be that, but for that madness, slavery would have gone as safely through Mr. Lincoln's administration as it had gone through that of Mr. Buchanan or any other. Slavery never rested on a firmer foundation than at the commencement of this war, which was inaugurated avowedly for the purpose of perpetuating it; but which, by a kind of retribution, apparently directed by Heaven, has destroyed it instead. It was indeed as secure as it was possible to make it *under our form of government.*

But therein precisely lay the main difficulty. The cause of our woes lurked *in the form of our government.* Without, perhaps, any man being able to account to himself satisfactorily for his want of faith, experience taught us all to *feel*, rather than to *understand*, the danger that threatened us from that quarter—a danger not the less fearful because vague and undefined and not fully understood. The South had some knowledge of the tumultuous, wild, capricious, and dangerous opinions of the Northern States,—their mobs, confusion, outbreaks, and incendiary doctrines,—which left nothing sacred, nothing secure, and which threatened the stability of all those pillars of society upon which man had been accustomed to lean in hope and safety: these dangerous influences the South had long suspected, and as long dreaded; she knew they must and would increase with the progress of time and the growth of population; she knew that population at the North was increasing with fearful rapidity, and that the bulk of that increase was of a character to render the licentious dogmas of democracy that much more disorganizing. Under these circumstances, she felt that a storm of some sort was brewing, and that her only safety was to be sought and found in her own conservative institutions. Where else could she hope to find protection from so many disorganizing influences? What was there in the nature of the Federal government calculated to inspire confidence that, in the hour of peril, it would be able to come to her rescue? The South knew that the government of the United States was a government of the numerical majority; that such a government must become, had already become, a government of party; and that in process of time that party must become, had already become, sectional, and influenced by sectional ideas and sectional interests. Under such conditions, with the doctrines of unbounded freedom of inquiry, of absolute popular sovereignty, universal suffrage, and universal equality as its fundamental principles, there was in the Southern mind a vague dread, an undefined apprehension of the utter insufficiency of the guarantees of the constitution, whenever the majority, in its character of absolute sovereignty, saw proper to break through its meshes. True, the majority was with the South to-day, but it was perhaps more from courtesy or policy than because it was real, and was liable at any moment to shift against her. The very facility with which amendments to the constitution were proposed and carried in her favor, was calculated to inspire dread rather than to reassure her.

Let us contemplate, for one moment, the melancholy instance of this superstitious fear which was afforded by the conduct of the Southern delegation during the last session of the 36th Congress. There sat in that fatal Congress, during that disastrous session, the bare nucleus of a party, a mere faction, few in numbers, stern as a decree of fate, and more appalling to Southern imaginations than the Archfiend himself, if he had just risen from Tophet to confront them. The Abolitionists, numerically insignificant as they then were, and deriving their chief importance from association with a larger faction, were regarded as composing the only growing party of the country, and as likely to be, at no distant day, the arbiters of the nation's destiny. Their late alliance with the Republicans, and the joint success they had just achieved, seemed to forestall their natural increase, and by a single bound to place them at once in possession of government. Animated by a fanaticism which, in one form or another, had always carried desolation over the earth and strewed the pages of history with narratives of wreck and ruin, they were deemed to be as resistless as they were known to be inexorable; hence the interest which was attached to their vote, and the terror which was felt at the uncompromising attitude of their hostility. As their vote never swerved in a single instance from their principles, and was steadily cast in opposition to every measure calculated to favor slavery, Southern members were deaf and blind to everything else transpiring around, and reckless of the immense majorities showered upon them, on all occasions, for their exclusive benefit. They made no account of the kind offices of their Northern friends to allay their fears. They heard nothing, saw nothing, but the "raw-head-and-bloody-bones" that sat before them and frowned upon their cause. They only knew the Abolitionists conceded nothing; all else was naught to them. This was childish terror, a senseless panic, which was inexcusable if it were real, and their conduct was still more reprehensible if it were affected. Nothing could be more erroneous than the opinions thus entertained of the then importance of the Abolitionists; or more groundless than the fears of the South, anticipating a future danger never likely to approach except by reason of her own folly. But, alas! how unfit were such men as Benjamin and Slidell, and others of that ilk, to encounter the horrid phantom their distempered imaginations had conjured up, or to meet in combat the feeble enemy into whose merciless power their fears or their treason contributed to deliver, naked and defenseless, a great and prosperous people!

How strange and inexplicable, except upon the grounds I have taken, has been the change so suddenly wrought in the peaceable relations of this country! As in the days of Nullification, there were no oppressions experienced under the old Union calling for an extreme measure like this: there were no invasions of public liberty, no ruin to private happiness, no long list of rights violated, or wrongs unredressed, to justify to history this wanton assault upon the free constitution of a free nation. At the time this work of dissolution and destruction was begun, the whole land lay smiling in peace and rejoicing in plenty. A general and high prosperity pervaded the country; and the South participated to the full in all those evidences of material abundance and national progress.

Assuredly, under such conditions, the South should not have been the first to throw away a constitution which, like the shield of Achilles, covered her all over, from head to foot; and which, whatever it might become thereafter, was at least impervious at that time. She should have held fast to that instrument as long as a fragment of it was left sufficient to hold by. If the constitution had to be violated, let others, if they chose to do so, commit the breach, and bear the responsibility of the guilty deed. So long as the constitution lasted, the South was in no danger; her interests could be reached only over its ruins; and beneath those ruins, by whomsoever caused, her society must be buried forever. It is a clear case, therefore, if she wished to preserve her institutions, that her battles, whether in hall or field, ought to have been fought under cover of its sacred ægis: she ought to have spent her last breath, her last drop of blood, if need were, in its defense; for, after Heaven, that constitution and the old flag were the only safeguards she possessed on this earth. While the whole world else was banded against her institution, the Federal constitution and the Federal government were straining every nerve for its protection. Nothing was wanting, on the part of her congressional representatives, but a little wise and temperate patriotism, a little courageous virtue, the heroism of conscious rectitude, to face the frowning specter which overcame them like the dread shadow of the future, and it would have vanished into thin air, never again perhaps to have been heard of.

By this judicious course, this patriotic and heroic conduct, four years would have been gained, perhaps many four years, which would have been of immense value to the South. If, after that epoch, the increase of the abolition vote *had* realized her fears, and given to that party a numerical preponderance which nothing else could have countervailed; and if fanaticism *had* at last broken down the bulwarks of the constitution, and committed an overt act of aggression against the South, through the constituted authorities of the General government,—then, in that case, the South would have been rendered morally and physically invincible, even in the questionable method of redress she so prematurely adopted. But even then she ought to have fought for the constitution, not against it: with that instrument in her hands, and beneath the old consecrated banner of the nation, it was clearly her policy and her duty to have gone forth as the peculiar champion of the Union, the constitution, and her rights under them. From such a vantage-ground, no argument, no after-reflection, no sober second thoughts could have driven her. She would *then* have united not only all the slave States in one unanimous and simultaneous coalition, but, against a provocation so indisputable, she would have enlisted the sympathies, perhaps the co-operation, certainly the approval, of Northern conservatives and the wise and just of the whole world. Against an opposing front so formidable, it is hardly probable this war would have been waged at all; but a peaceable revolution instead might have rectified all causes of complaint, and established the integrity of the Union, upon an enduring basis, for an indefinite period to come.

Such a course, however, so patriotic and so judicious, would have gone far to demonstrate the capacity of the people for self-government, and to justify the establishment of society upon the basis of an exclusive democracy and the federative system. But the truth was, and is, that not one in ten of the Southern people knew, or yet knows, anything of the real facts of the case. They believed, and still believe, many of them, that Mr. Lincoln and the Northern people were pledged to the immediate abolition of slavery and the ruin of the South; and that now the Abolitionists had acquired the reins of government, they possessed the power to carry out their wicked purposes, and would inevitably do so. The demagogues, if they knew better, instead of correcting this misconception of the people, encouraged it rather, and did all in their power to aggravate the evil and precipitate the crisis. And thus it was that ignorance and knavery, as personified in the majority, and acting through the functions of government, have been mainly instrumental in bringing about this wide-spread ruin for no adequate cause whatever. All the facts which have led to this disastrous war demonstrate the unfitness of the democratic principles, in the present state of civilization, to reign alone at the foundation of government, and still more the unfitness of a federative system like this to bind together innumerable States possessed of populations so little qualified to deal with the intricate problems implicated in its general form and structure. In such a government, order may prevail for years, and flatter the patriot with an apparent realization of his fondest hopes of social perfection; but a day or an hour shall come at last, which will

20*

balk the calculation of years, and terminate forever the hopes of the philanthropist.

But it is useless to push conjectures and arguments further in this direction. We can know nothing now with *certainty* as to what might or might not have taken place, if a different course had been pursued. What we *do* know, with only too much certainty, is the stern reality of the horrors that now beset us. That something *better* might have been devised, we can well conceive; but how anything *worse* could have been hit upon, it is difficult to imagine. If there had been any just cause for secession and its inevitable consequences, or if the pretended causes which the Southern people so gratuitously assumed had really existed, then one could submit with patience and even exultation to the cruel sacrifices hourly demanded by the demon of destruction. In that case, the noble heroisms which, on the part of the South, already decorate the annals of the war, and hang like garlands around her armies, would give such an earnest of success that the faintest heart might well grow bold in the confidence of ultimate triumph. Emulous of so much glory, cased in the triple armor of a righteous quarrel, *and fighting for that which was attainable*, not one of her sons but would march with undoubting faith to her banner, as to the *oriflamme* of Liberty, and proudly conquer beneath its folds, or as proudly die in its defense.

As it is, we can lay no such flattering unction to our souls. The justice of our cause was not beyond the reach of doubt: we did not even complain of any grievance unredressed: the oppressions against which we rebelled were not flagrant,—they were prospective only,

they existed merely in possibility, and might or might not have taken place: those outrageous tyrannies which drive a generous people into revolt were, in our case, not even inchoations. Happy at home, respected abroad, enjoying a degree of liberty and prosperity never experienced by any people before, our glorious country has been plunged into the depths of misery by the wanton spirit of a licentious democracy. Impelled by the instincts of an unmitigated selfishness, intolerant of law or order, we have trapped ourselves in a dilemma we cannot escape, either horn of which is sufficient to gore us to death. For if we gain our independence, we shall gain only ruin in the end, since we must inevitably perish by the principles for which we are contending; if, on the other hand, we are vanquished—we must call on the gods for mercy, not on abolitionism. Thus are we sacrificing the lives of our brave and generous youths fighting for—we know not what.

Alas! what do I say? Mr. Lincoln has at last, since the war began, furnished us with a pretext. He alone, as the organ of abolitionism, could have afforded secession a plausible excuse for prolonging a strife so causelessly begun. His ill-advised proclamation, as unjust as it was impolitic, was alone wanting to convert a wanton rebellion into a defensive contest, and to enlist the heart and patriotism of the entire South in a life-and-death struggle for her just rights. Secession now points to Mr. Lincoln's abolition war policy as a verification of its worst fears; congratulates its sagacity in having penetrated so long beforehand into the lurking designs of its wily enemy; triumphantly proclaims that the war was not begun a day too soon; and truly declares that the Southern people have now no choice but to fight on, so long as the present policy is adhered to.

Thus do we travel in a vicious circle, from which it seems impossible to escape. Caught up in a whirlpool, made by the action and reaction upon each other of two evil principles, we are carried on, nearing each moment a vortex which must engulf us at last, unless rescued by some power not now visible to mortal eye. Secession, as if envious of the national prosperity, made haste to mar so much happiness, and, with reckless indifference to consequences, precipitated the country into a calamity too frightful to contemplate. A generous forbearance practiced long enough; a continued prosecution of the war upon constitutional principles, without the aid of abolitionism; a magnanimous policy persisted in to the last; a scrupulous, even a tender, respect for the persons, the rights, the property of non-combatants; an unwearied perseverance in pursuing a course so lofty, so chivalrous, would, at a comparatively early day, have achieved an easy triumph over the outrageous revolt of the lawless principle of secession. The South herself, if sufficient time had been allowed her under the milder treatment of a constitutional regimen, would have recovered her reason and corrected her error much sooner than she is likely to do under existing circumstances. Her own reflection, undisturbed by subsequent provocations, would have contributed more than all the armies of the North to the speedy cure of her temporary aberration. A better opportunity could not have occurred to prove, by example, to the South that the North had no evil designs upon her institution; that in spite even of a provocation so flagrant as that of secession, the latter was still determined to hold by the constitution, and save the Union by it alone, or perish with it in the conflict. This would have been the sublimity of human virtue, and the very dignity of true manhood. An example so lofty, conduct so disinterested, could not have failed, sooner or later, to excite the emulation of the South, convince her of her error, and win her back to a sense of duty. It would have bound her heart in the chains of love, respect, and gratitude; and insured a happy reunion cemented by the ties of cordiality and good-will. This is the more probable, because there were thousands of the best men in the South who never gave their consent to secession from the first; and, though overborne for the moment by the clamors of ignorance and passion, were quietly working a slow but sure reaction in public sentiment in favor of the Union.

But this happy rectification was not destined to so easy an accomplishment. Different counsels prevailed. Political mountebanks were at the helm of State. Secession had a worthy rival in the field, offspring of the same polity, which could not afford to lose an opportunity so favorable for a little sharp practice of its own in the way of mischief making. It was the very occasion, aptly prepared to its hand, which abolitionism had been so long watching and praying for; and now that secession, as if demented by the gods, had blindly fallen into the trap, no excuse must be afforded for its escape thence. And thus, between the two, a carnival of death is instituted, where demons preside, and at which humanity shudders.

It is in vain for the South to plead this after-act of abolitionism in justification of her first offense. The initiative was hers: she inaugurated the war; and history cannot hold her innocent of the crimes now enacting on her soil. A consciousness of imprudence, of precipitancy, if not of guilt, must disturb her peace of mind amid her victories and defeats. God was not in the wind, nor the earthquake, nor the fire which passed by Elijah in Horeb's mount; but after these came a *still small voice*, which was the divinity that spoke within him. So must it be with the South in this day of retribution. The God of vengeance is passing by; but there is no deity in the slaughters of her battle-fields: they are evidences of the divine wrath instead. Amid these, the whispers of any uneasy conscience must make themselves heard above the din of arms, suggesting, with their *still small voice*, that "Perhaps all was not done for the best: the blood of our sons might have been spared: their lives, after all, may have been sacrificed to a mistake: a little more prudence, forethought, forbearance, and these ensanguined plains, now red with the blood of so many noble hearts fallen in vain, might have been blooming with the harvests of life! And who are they that were appointed to think for us, to advise us, to lead us, and who could conduct us only to this ruin, to these bloody graves?" Ah, my countrymen! it is a fearful thing to know that many thousand voices are daily ascending to heaven, crying, with sobs and breaking hearts, for vengeance on such multitudinous crimes, or for errors little short of crimes! Reflecting men should think twice, and hesitate long, before plunging a nation in such wholesale calamity: *statesmen* are not needed for this work of destruction—savages would do it as well.

The amnesty of war has been most inconsiderately proclaimed by a shallow philosophy, on the ground of the great benefits which result from it to humanity and civilization. This is nothing more than a justification of the means by the end, supposing the opinion to be true. But war is a huge evil, and man is not permitted to do evil that good may come of it. It is the province of God only to bring good out of evil. "It cannot be but that evil shall be done in the world, and that good will come of it, but woe be unto the evil-doer," is the denunciation of Heaven. There is nothing which can happen in this world, however disastrous for the moment, but a benefit of some sort will grow out of it, sooner or later, to some one or other, simply because good necessarily comes of all things. But only fools or madmen will purposely bring wreck and ruin on the present in order that some unknown future advantage may haply spring thence. The present is wisely enjoined to take the best possible care of itself, and leave the future to do the same: if, in spite of the utmost precaution to stave off the evil, the future derive any benefit from the unavoidable misfortunes of the present, nothing is to be said against it. War is an abnormal condition of society: it seldom fails to inflict signal vengeance on those who bring it about, or are engaged in it: it is the shirt of Nessus, the gift of a malignant spirit to those who invoke it: it is the destruction of all social order, while it lasts, and the relentless enemy of the present. The benefits which flow from it to the future are no doubt consolations to posterity, but very inadequate compensations to the immediate sufferers: it is poor consolation to the victims of the middle ages that we, at this day, are reaping the advantages of their bloody wars. Men never divide except upon the elements of error: about the truth there can be no difference of opinion: in every aspect of truth, all must coincide; for truth is the faithful expression of reality. Wherever there is dissension, disagreement, there is error. It has often been said that both sides of a quarrel cannot be right; that one at least must be wrong: it is nearer the truth to say that both are wrong. War, therefore, must always be absurd; for it is only error which causes the combat, and nothing but evil can come of it to the combatants. The very existence of war is *prima facie* evidence that there is a great wrong somewhere, of which it is the retribution. War never occurs where right and equity, good sense and love of truth, prevail; for these make us tolerant. Internecine wars are the necessary concomitants of a corrupt society and a feeble government. A weak government indeed is the greatest crime which can be committed against society; and it is sure to bring its own punishment, in the shape of endless revolutions, as long as it lasts.

The frantic intolerance which seized the Southern mind at the announcement of Mr. Lincoln's election, and the hot haste with which the entire population flew to arms and challenged the North to combat, as the only mode of redress they would accept, even before it was certain there was anything to redress, affords an instance of those moral epidemics, or national insanities, which happen periodically in even the best-regulated nations. Nothing can more clearly indicate the necessity of a strong government, well guarded at every point, than the certain recurrence of those perilous moments which, when they do happen, tear to pieces a feeble government such as ours was, and consign to ruin an entire generation, perhaps the nation itself. If the government be strong enough to resist the first onset, time will be afforded for reflection, and the danger will pass away with the return of reason and sober thoughts. The people, when acting in multitudes, are always impulsive, inexorably cruel and reckless; but they are also as cowardly as they are cruel, because, being as yet unorganized, they know their weakness, and readily yield to a disciplined force when promptly directed against them with merciless vigor. If the government be too weak to meet thus the first-shock, time will be afforded the insurgents for organization, and civil war ensues.

If the government of the United States had possessed any portion of this so much needed strength and energy, the mania of the Southern people would have been innoxious, and order had prevailed to this day. But the doctrine of State rights was stronger than the Federal government; and it was precisely the vigor of the former which had caused the feebleness of the latter. The sentiment of contempt which had always been entertained for the Federal authority, when weighed against the sovereignty of the States, was not calculated to breed in the Southern mind that salutary fear of the power of government which, if it had existed, would have effectually restrained any manifestation of its disorganizing proclivities. The fatal ease with which the South knew or thought she could accomplish her ideas of secession, contributed as much as anything else to plunge the country into this vortex. This was no doubt one, perhaps foremost, among many other moving causes; but also the cruel sympathy of Mr. Buchanan's administration, and the no less cruel tenderness and dilly-dallying of Mr. Lincoln's initiatory proceedings,—both of them results of an insufficient government,—cannot be held entirely innocent of aiding and abetting to fix the movement and to bring it to a head. At least, whatever difference of opinion may be entertained of the complicity of the two latter, there can be none as to that of the former.

The doctrine of State rights had been too long *preached* in the South, not to be practiced there some time or other; it was too great a favorite to be kept suspended and held in abeyance forever; the time was at last come for it to manifest its quality, to show that it was as terrible in action as it was sublime in repose, and that it possessed all the *practical* efficiency that was *theoretically* claimed for it. So incontestable appeared the doctrine of State sovereignty, and the concurrent right of the States peaceably to quit the Union when they pleased, that few men in the South believed a gun would be fired against secession. It was inconceivable to them that a principle, which was cotemporaneous with the existence of the nation, which was laid down by Mr. Calhoun, and the justice of which could be deduced, past all manner of doubt, from the terms of the *compact*, should be disputed at this late day—and by whom? By the Federal government? Why, the Federal government was nothing but a creature of the States; the latter had created it, and, by their sovereign will and pleasure, could dissolve it. It was a mere partnership concern, voluntarily entered into by independent States for certain specified purposes; and because the States went into it voluntarily, they could go out of it at their option.

As for the claims of civilization, the right of humanity to stable government and permanent security, the inviolability of laws, and the reform of abuses by legal means, —these things were little considered, and scarcely even thought of by the many. The sentiment which dominated most minds was a sense of lawless liberty, the unrestrained freedom of doing as they pleased with their own; this indeed was a *natural right* which belonged as well to States as to individuals, and as such was inalienable, and admitted of no qualifications; it was always held in reserve for fit occasions, suspended, not abolished; and the time was come for it to resume the rude vigor of its *feræ naturæ.* If all other arguments fail, the law of revolution remains; that right at least is indisputable. The right of resistance, which was instituted by their forefathers, and constitutes the glory of those good old times, had come down to them unimpaired, and should suffer no deterioration in their hands. Their hearts and their arms were as stout as those of their ancestors, and should re-enact the splendors of the past. Welcome, then, the sacrament of death! for of no value is a nation until baptized with blood.

Such were some of the ideas that presided at the grand national saturnalia of secession which was celebrated with so much *eclat* down South little more than two years ago. It was, in a somewhat modified form, one of those orgies of liberty which have characterized every epoch of modern history, since the introduction upon its stage of those barbarians that sacked the Roman world, and erected upon its ruins empires of their own.

A leading trait of those savage tribes was a sentiment of personal independence, a love of individual liberty, displaying itself without regard to consequences, and with scarcely any other aim than its own satisfaction. This element of their untamed nature they introduced into modern civilization. It was an element unknown among the Romans, and is scarcely perceptible in any of the civilizations of antiquity. "The liberty we meet with in ancient civilizations," says Guizot, "is political liberty. It was not about his personal liberty that man troubled himself, it was about his liberty as a citizen. He formed part of an association, and to this alone he was devoted." The liberty which the barbarian engrafted on modern civilization was quite a different affair: it was personal, individual freedom; the right to do as he pleased with himself and all that belonged to him; the pleasure of enjoying in full force and liberty all his powers of mind and body, without being obliged to render an account to any one of his conduct. It is from these barbarous hordes, which overran the old Roman empire, that are derived the populations of all modern European nations. The base of this population is derived from the most sturdy, independent, licentious, and turbulent of those old barbarians, to wit, the old Norse and Scandinavian tribes, the vikings and sea-rovers of early times, nature's democrats, as they have since been called. Their wild nature has never been entirely eliminated from their descendants to this day; the same turbulence, the same licentiousness, the same sense of independence are yet latent in their nature; and however those traits of character may slumber for a time, they still break forth on every suitable occasion.

The same is true of the element of personal freedom which they introduced into modern civilization, and which is so conspicuous in this society: that social element has not yet been wholly tamed down to the gentle restraints of law and order, nor has it yet been fully assimilated by conversion into institutions. The one is not yet the civilized man, nor the other the civilized principle, complete. The social natures of both require to be further developed before society can be perfected by them. In view of these elements of our population and society, the restraints of force, of a strong government, and a vigorous discipline are more needed and exist to a less extent here than in any nation in the world.

Hence, then, the character of the ideas, enumerated above, which were mainly instrumental in hurrying the Southern people into their rash and unpremeditated revolution; they were identical with the democratic principles which have been implicated in so many similar revolutions in Europe, and which finally established themselves at the foundation of this government, and are only just now beginning to break out into their old accustomed revolts and to seek the gratification of their natural desire for war. Of course the Southern mind was, to some degree, influenced by other ideas of a graver character, which possessed more dignity and truth, and were entitled to more respect. I have only marked these to show the extent to which the public mind can be demoralized by a set of loose and disjointed principles acting for any length of time through the functions of government; and also to show how little stability and security can be looked for in a government where they prevail.

The love of individual liberty is a precious sentiment which should never be absent from any nation or government; it has produced lasting benefits wherever it has existed; and it is to be hoped that it will never depart from the heart of man, nor ever become *functus officio* in society. The right of resistance, which flows directly from the above sentiment, is a sacred right which no sane man can wish to see abolished. If that principle were erased from the mind of society, it would be prepared to put on the shackles of servitude. But any government is radically vicious in which the right of resistance, however incontestable it may be in the *abstract*, is not *practically* rendered forever inactive and useless. Inasmuch as it is a *natural* right, an imperishable instinct of human nature, and cannot be ignored *socially*, it is the duty of society to absorb it, that is, to incorporate it into its own artificial structure, into free institutions, that is, again, to organize it and supply it with laws. Thus regulated, and armed with the full legalized power of the State, it needs not to break out into arbitrary acts and brute violence; it would have no occasion for revolutions; it would completely inutilize civil wars; it would become at once a moral and social force of the first magnitude; and would guarantee the stability of society by insuring the execution of justice legally. This is the great end, the chief perfection, of social order.

There is a wide difference between this legal resistance, judicially established in the frame of a well-regulated society, and that lawless resistance which springs arbitrarily from individual wills, or from the caprices of opinion, with or without legitimate provocation, of which it is the sole self-constituted and self-sufficient arbiter. It is clear that, where this right exists and can be exercised at pleasure, there is no security for anybody or anything; no legal right can coexist with it; it is a terrible antisocial right, inasmuch as its only appeal is to brute force, to war, which is the destruction of society itself.

Such was the nature of the resistance inaugurated by secession at the South. But it was called into action by conduct no less arbitrary, lawless, and reprehensible at the North. Abolitionism is not a whit less guilty than secession. One was the inevitable consequence of the other; and both resulted from the fundamental principles of the government. If abolitionism has a right to exist at the North, secession has a right to exist at the South: one follows the other as a logical corollary. To suppress forcibly secession at the South, while abolitionism is allowed to prevail at the North; nay, to employ the latter to sit in judgment upon and punish the former; to allow one guilty principle to arraign, try, convict, and execute sentence upon a not more guilty adversary, is a despotism of so vile a character that human nature shudders at the very thought of it. If one of these principles is wrong, both are wrong; and that both are wrong is a fact as evident as the fact of the war which they have produced, or of which they have been the occasion. If the calamities which this war is causing, and the desolation it is bringing on the country, are moral and material benefits, then must abolitionism and secession be accounted virtues of the first water. But if the tree in this case be judged by its fruits, and the latter are so bitter, then how is it possible for the good men and true of both sides to look on the infernal confusion which these two devilish principles are producing, and not make some effort to consign them to their place below? If they were angels and ministers of grace, and brought with them airs from heaven, and not blasts from hell, as they are doing, they could not be more tolerated in their respective sections than they seem to be. Nero fiddled while Rome was burning. The nation is bleeding to death, and not a finger is lifted to stop the effusion of blood. Those who are not fighting like wild beasts, are preying like harpies on the vitals of the land, and think only of turning its misfortunes to their profit. Or, peradventure, like Sodom and Gomorrah, the nation is given up to its fate, because there are not good men enough in it to save it. Of the ease and rapidity with which society can be broken up and man degenerate toward the savage state, the South is now a most melancholy illustration; her present condition is a transient return to barbarism, and clearly attests the barbaric origin of the people. But if this much can be said of the South, what less can be said of the Goths and Vandals who have so needlessly wrought all this desolation? Their footsteps can be traced by the ruins they have left wherever they have gone; and their cruelties and spoliations attest how little they have derived from their boasted civilization and the benevolent teachings of Christianity.

In any case, if we would have peace and order restored and society revived, let justice, first of all, be done on every side; for without it, it is in vain to hope for peace, or order, or anything but strife and confusion.

Therefore, before secession can be justly called on to lay down its arms, it must be shown that abolitionism has been suppressed, or at least relegated from the head of government. For, I repeat, how monstrous it is for one guilty principle to be placed in the chair of State to judge and punish an accomplice perhaps less guilty, certainly not more so, than itself! The perpetration, under existing circumstances, of such an instance of injustice as the establishment of practical abolitionism into a principle of government, and even seating it in the Presidential chair, is equivalent to a consecration of endless rebellion. One wrong is generally the fruitful parent of many more. Other instances of injustice cannot fail to spring up by the side of one so flagrant, and in the end the perpetual revolt of society will be a co-ordinate branch of government.

Such a state of things would by no means be a social novelty. It would not be the first time society was established on the basis of popular resistance. This condition, to which we appear to be drifting, would be exactly analogous to the social organization of the FREE CITIES of Europe in the eleventh and twelfth centuries. Those cities constituted the most marked feature of European civilization at that epoch; their society resembled our own in more respects than one; and the resemblance is fast becoming still more striking. Their government consisted of two very simple elements—the general assembly of all the inhabitants, and a magistracy invested with almost arbitrary power, *under the responsibility and surveillance of general insurrections.* These popular outbreaks were the only guarantees of good government; they passed into a co-ordinate branch of the constitutional organization of the corporations, and were as confidently looked for, and as constantly made their appearance, as any other municipal regulation. Guided as they were by the blind, licentious, furious spirit of democracy, they soon put an end to all security, and consigned the *Free Cities*, like feudalism, to absorption by monarchy and the great empires.

When I assert that abolitionism is directly responsible for secession, and make it equally guilty of the war, there may seem to be a contradiction, in my argument, with the previous declaration, and even proof, that secession was purely gratuitous and uncalled for. It is true that secession, as a general principle, depends not for its existence on abolitionism, or anything else exclusively; but as it lurks in the fundamental principles of society, and there is nothing in the form of government to prevent it, it is liable to break out at any moment, on any provocation, or no provocation at all. Nevertheless, in the present instance abolitionism did precede secession, waked it in its lair, roused its fury, and by a thousand taunts and threats gave direction to its rage by making it believe,—whether falsely or not makes no difference, since it was done on purpose, with malice aforethought and with evil intent,—by making it believe, I say, that the darling institution it was invoked to protect was in danger of extinction. Whether or not the demagogues knew better than this is doubtful; but if a few intelligent men were better posted, the majority of the people were not, and were conscientious in their belief of the wrongs intended them. It was the ignorant majority, therefore, a fundamental feature of the government and its very mainspring, which, in this instance, did the mischief. The South is notoriously thin-skinned on the subject of slavery, and is ready to take alarm at anything that wears the semblance of danger that way. Her fears once excited, she is as prompt and fierce in defense of her institution as a tigress of her cubs, and not more discriminating. If her discretion had been equal to her valor, the latter would have been less exercised than it has been of late. This blind impulse is further intensified, and perhaps rendered more belligerent than it might otherwise be, by the reputation the Southern people have somehow or other acquired of being the descendants of "Cavaliers,"—not of "Roundheads," like the Northern people,—and of possessing all the "chivalry" of the land. Some fool has told them this, and they have no better sense than to believe it. The belief, whether well or ill founded, makes them as ready to fight as to eat, not because there is any necessity for it, or because they have more stomach that way than others, but because they think it incumbent on them to support their character of being regular Boanergeses, (sons of thunder.) The shrewd abolitionists, aware of this weakness, goaded them on to a practical assertion of it by the most bitter taunts they could think of: they told them their chivalry was nothing but gas; that "they could not be kicked out of the Union;" dared them to try to leave it, and they would soon be kicked back; and then there was something about "blue cockades" being as scarce as "blue roses" round about Charleston as soon as a United States frigate made its appearance there, or something to that effect. This childish nonsense had more effect than one would suppose: it was more than so much puerile vanity and conceit could stand: like a parcel of school-boys they had been *dared*, and at once determined that it was unbecoming "Southern chivalry" to take a dare from a set of canting, puritanical snobs: the prick-eared knaves should "be made to feel Southern steel and smell Southern powder," etc.

This may seem a rather ridiculous analysis of secession; but trivial as these causes appear, when predicated of a great nation waging gigantic wars, and marching majestically along the grand highway of history, they were not without their influence, and ought not to be overlooked; nor are they more puerile than the motives which have ever influenced mankind in the production of history through all past ages. When dramatically written, and carefully winnowed of the personalities, passions, vanities, and base motives, which are always the secondary or immediate causes of its details, history reads very loftily, and gives one sublime ideas of the dignity of human nature. But history, too, has its grotesque and vulgar side, its ridiculous and comic aspect. M. Cousin has said something like this; and he has also said there are no *individuals* in great wars and battles, only their *causes* appear there. But the cotemporary, the actual spectator, sees nothing else but individuals: they crowd the stage of history and fill the fields of battle, they and their miserable little passions; and, however *trivialities* may vanish from the *philosophy* of history, they alone occupy its *annals*. We may also learn from this analysis that the majority of men, whatever they may become hereafter, are yet little more than grown-up children; and if society is ever destined to escape the inconveniences arising from their unruly impulses, they must still be subjected to the discipline of a species of government not greatly dissimilar from that exercised over children.

Now, if the South had felt that confidence in the capacity and inclination of the Federal government to protect her interest, which every government ought to inspire in its subjects, it is hardly probable she would have resorted to arms to protect herself. And it is unquestionably true that if the government had possessed the requisite amount of strength, and been dispossessed of its party character, abolitionism never could have culminated to that summit of power at which the South became so alarmed; and, in all probability, neither abolitionism nor secession had ever been heard of. The South, therefore, should no more be held to a criminal accountability for secession than the North for abolitionism; for it is well known the Abolitionists advocated the same measure as a means of accomplishing their unconstitutional designs, and were only prevented from carrying it into execution by the want of strength to do so. "The Union," to use their own words, "was a league with hell and a compact with the devil," and the sooner it could be made to "slide," the better. Hence the insults they heaped upon the Southern people, and their successful efforts in making the latter a cat's-paw to effect their own ruin. If secession, therefore, be a capital offense, as no doubt it is, the plea of *se defendendo* is clearly admissible in extenuation of punishment. In any case, the Abolitionists ought to be the last to bring accusations against it. To be consistent and just, they ought to recuse the case; and common sense and common equity would sustain the recusation.

But granting secession to have been an anachronism,

and therefore wrong, when it was first instituted as a means of self-defense, because the South was not then directly assailed by any overt act of aggression, and because it was unknown what might or might not have been the future policy of Mr. Lincoln's administration, the subsequent adoption by that administration of the abolition programme changes the entire aspect of the case. The indorsement by the Federal government of the abolition policy, as manifested in its conduct of the war, no matter from what cause it was made, puts the South legitimately on the defensive, and keeps it there as long as its rights are thus assaulted. Leaving out of view altogether the constitutionality of the question, and the belligerent right of "military necessity," the question resolves itself into one of a predetermined policy, a foregone conclusion; and the nature of this policy, of this predetermination, depends entirely upon the *animus* of the Federal administration and of the Northern people. What, then, is the ulterior purpose, the principal aim, of the Federal administration? Is the purpose a single one, or does it include the accomplishment of more than one design in the same end? And does the administration, in the adoption of that purpose, whatever it may be, single or multiple, truly represent the wishes of the Northern people? Is it the design of the administration, first of all, to make use of the war as a suitable occasion, aptly prepared to its hand, for the abolition of slavery, as a prime consideration and end to be achieved for its own sake? And is it further the purpose of the administration to confiscate the property of the South, or any portion of it? or to deprive her of any of her political rights? or to inflict any other species of punishment upon the Southern people, or upon any portion of them? If these be the fell purposes of the administration, and they accord with the wishes of the Northern people, then there is nothing more to be said about it. If they have the power to execute these designs, to carry out such purposes, to accomplish such wishes, no one of course can prevent them; the might, in this case, gives the right. But, then, it is clear this foregone policy of the Federal government must also predetermine the course of the Southern people. Their all is at stake; and their enemy leaves them no choice but, win or lose, to stand the hazard of the die: they must take counsel only of necessity, derive their inspiration from a single alternative, and, with the generous courage of a noble despair, die with arms in their hands; and that they will thus dare to die, who that knows them will dare to doubt?

From this view of the case it follows that, though originally in the wrong, the South has changed places with the Federal government, and is actually forced, by the policy of the latter, to continue the war as long as she can. While her dearest interests are assailed, and the very existence of her society and of everything she possesses in the world is threatened, the South is deprived, by the peculiar attitude of the Federal government, of even the ability, much more the inclination, to enter into any compromise looking to a restoration of the Union under the constitution: because such a compromise would be nothing else but a compact with her avowed enemy, who, in making it, surrenders no aggressive right, but maintains the same hostile posture to the last. It would be the dictation of dishonorable terms by a conqueror to a conquered people. It would be to restore the Union without the equal benefits of the Union. It would be to reinstate the constitution without conceding to the South an equal participation in the rights conferred by the constitution. It would be, in short, only a miserable parologism, a contradiction of terms, a conclusion unauthorized by the premises, false in logic, false in principle, false, above all, to that magnanimous nobility of nature which should characterize a great and free people, who, loving liberty for its own sake, should scorn to impose servile terms upon their erring brothers. Rather let the fatted calf be killed in honor of the returning prodigals, and the past be forgiven and forgotten in a cordial reunion of hearts as well as of States; or if the past must be remembered at all, let it be remembered only to correct the errors which have led to such disastrous results.

But there is one other consequence which flows from this policy of the Federal government and the Northern people—if such indeed be their policy. By its adoption of practical abolitionism, as manifested in its conduct of the war,—to say nothing of the wholesale confiscation which is threatened,—the administration at Washington ceases to be a General government of the entire nation, constitutionally administered upon principles of equal and impartial justice, and degenerates into—what was a foregone conclusion of the democratic principles—purely and exclusively a government of party. It was equally conclusive from the first that this ruling party must ultimately become purely sectional, residing in a particular portion of the common country rather than in another, favoring the peculiar interest of that section, and of course become antagonistic to some other interest, which it must in time destroy. It is precisely to this point our politics have at last arrived, on the supposition of the foregoing policy being adhered to and fully carried out; and this war must be considered as being the last term, the necessary consequence of the fundamental principles of this government. As long, then, I repeat, as her present belligerent attitude is forced upon her by the continuance of these facts, the South has no choice but to carry on the war to the last extremity; and if she must perish by superior force, she will at least perish with her harness on, and fighting like a nation that deserves to be free.

To disarm secession, therefore, or to put it in the wrong and keep it there, it is first of all incumbent on the Washington administration to plant itself immovably on the constitution, disavow abolitionism, and by its method of conducting the war afford the South no pretext for a longer continuance of her disorganizing behavior. This change of war-policy on the part of the Federal administration will be a prelude to other things: it will be the first note of a summons to parley: it will prepare the Southern mind to listen to the voice of reason, and return to a sense of duty, a duty it owes to itself, to the nation, to humanity, to civilization. The concession thus far will be mutual, and the pride or honor or interests of neither party need be considered as having been compromised. The Federal government at least will have rectified its error, will have made the *amende honorable;* and if the South, after her bitter experience, refuse to meet advances thus made in the spirit of candor and good fellowship, she must bear the responsibility of whatever consequences may follow her contumacy. But it is not anticipated by those who know the state of the public mind at the South, that if the foregoing conditions be fulfilled by the Federal government, any serious difficulty will remain in the way of reconciliation.

Conclusion.

I will not encumber these pages with specifications of organic changes which may seem to be required by the general welfare in the structure of government. I have already said enough to indicate the general character of those alterations which, in my opinion, are peremptorily demanded, not perhaps as prerequisites of a reconstruction of the Union, but as indispensable to its perpetuity thereafter. It is not for me to particularize those changes. I shall not endanger the favorable reception of these remarks by descending to minutias, about which all minds may disagree. It is for the assembled wisdom of the nation to determine what those fundamental modifications shall be, and to introduce such specific innovations into the form of our government as the nature of the case may seem to require.

That those necessary alterations will ever be voluntarily made, or this war suddenly arrested and a peaceable reconstruction of the Union effected by compromise, is more than the most sanguine dare hope for. If it should be so, it will be the first time in the history of the world that a great revolution has been arrested in mid career, and turned back upon itself, by the wise forethought of the very persons who began it. Such an achievement would be the glory of the age, and the triumph of civilization over the passions of mankind. It would proclaim the approach of a social science destined to illumine the world, and to countermand revolutions for all time to come.

But this is almost too bright a vision for the human imagination to indulge. It is to be feared the time is not yet come for so much illumination, and that this revolution must run the usual career of violence and bloodshed. There is something deeply melancholy in the contemplation of a spectacle so fraught with ruin and desolation brought on themselves by men who aim only at realizing their ideas of social order. But in all great events of this kind, how many ignorant and "disastrous efforts must be made, before the successful one!" Human ignorance is the fruitful source of all the woes that afflict human society. It is sad to see a great nation, like a sightless Polyphemus, deprived of the light of reason, hurling destruction around, because it knows not what else to do, what it wants, or how to right its wrongs. Helpless in our ignorance, we can only weep over so much heroism wasted, so much blind effort misdirected, so much brute force abused. But is not the loss of so much courage, of so many sacrifices and endeavors, of so much virtue, a sorrowful sight? It is true, as Guizot remarks of these revolutions, that Providence, upon all such occasions, in order to accomplish His designs, is prodigal of courage, virtues, sacrifices—finally of man; and it is only after a vast number of ignorant attempts apparently lost—after a host of noble hearts have fallen into despair—convinced that their cause was ruined—that it triumphs at last.

Such has ever been the nature of the painful progress of society through the dreary ages of the past. Revolution after revolution, each apparently more disastrous than the other, have brought it thus far forward on its bloody path, only to consign it, alas! to another, which still repeats the sad story of man's endless failures to realize his ideas of order and happiness. This is what is called the spontaneous development of civilization, directed solely by the blind forces of nature. But there is another species of development,—it is the reflective method by which the social evolution unfolds itself, guided by reason and the wise forethought of enlightened statesmen, and an intelligent community who study social laws, and by their knowledge of them give to civilization the direction it wishes to take.

At an earlier period, the very existence of laws which were perpetually transforming society in spite of itself was not even suspected; hence the blind struggles, the fruitless efforts, the ruinous endeavors that were made to resist them. But now we know more than was known then; and it is our disgrace and our punishment that we make so little use of this knowledge. We thrust forward presumptuous demagogues, whom we call statesmen, and seem not to know that our ills are come of their ignorance. The eagles being retired from our political sky, these birds of night come forth, and brood all our woes. When, therefore, our errors recoil upon ourselves, and we know not what else to do, we fall to cutting each other's throats. This we call statesmanship; and our great men are they who can do only this.

If the foregoing remarks have disclosed anything, they have discovered to us the "danger, the evil, the insurmountable vice of absolute power." It matters not where this power may reside, whether in one man or in many, in a monarch or a majority, in a king or the people; nor by whatsoever name it may be called, whether a theocracy, an aristocracy, a monarchy, or a democracy,—its effects in every case are the same; and it is never otherwise than destructive of the main ends for which society is established. Wherever a single principle controls the movement of society, there tyranny is inevitable; for nothing is more complex than social interests, and if but one principle be allowed at the basis of government, then only one interest will be represented, which will dominate all others. It is the duty, and should be the peculiar event of our time, to recognize the important fact that all power, whether belonging to governments or people, bears within itself a natural vice, a tendency to abuse, is accompanied with an almost invincible craving to exercise and diffuse itself, which call for the most stringent limitations that human ingenuity can impose upon it. In systems of government, the only method of limiting political forces is by admitting all principles, interests, rights, to a full representation in the frame of society; to give to all these "a free manifestation and legal existence;" and to so adjust all that they shall check and balance, without destroying each other. "Nothing but a system which insures all this, can restrain every particular force or power within its legitimate bounds, and prevent it from encroaching on the others." This is one social law with which we are now well acquainted; and we know equally well that such are not the terms of our social system; but that democracy reigns there alone, and tyrannizes every other interest.

We have also discovered, in the course of this investigation, one other fact of no little importance. We have learned that principles of order and progress should coexist in the same social system; that both security and movement, stability and advancement, conservatism and amelioration are essential to social existence. Every system which contains not this double advantage, this compound virtue, is vicious, incompetent, and is speedily abandoned. Any system, to be permanent, must provide for order for the present and progress for the future. We are but too well aware that our social system is not built upon this plan: that its foundation is too narrow: although it pretends to be founded upon the broad basis of the whole people, it is not so in reality, for there is but one force, one interest, one principle of human nature there. We know, therefore, we cannot but know, that the failure of our system is due to the absence of general interests and general ideas: that everything about it is, as yet, too special, too individual, too local: that its government of the majority is nothing else but the government of party: that this party government must ultimately become purely sectional: that the federative compact is nothing but a system of voluntary obedience, which is equivalent to no obedience at all: that the policy of the government depends at all times upon the caprices of individual opinions: that at this very moment the government is lending itself to the passions of fanaticism; and that, finally, a long and powerful process of centralization is needed, before our society can become at once extensive, solid, and regular—objects which all societies necessarily seek to attain.

The only parallel to this state of things which the history of modern times affords is that of Italy; and the condition of utter decomposition to which we are hastening renders the parallel all the closer and the lesson it teaches so much the more instructive. I cannot do better here than to close these remarks by a quotation from M. Guizot's able work on the History of European Civilization, in which he so well describes the melancholy condition of Italy, arising mainly from the same causes which are about to subject our unhappy country to a similar fate. The quotation will be found at pages 220, 221 of the second volume, edited in this country by Professor Henry, of the University of the City of New York.

"In looking at the history of the Italian republics, from the eleventh to the fifteenth century, we are struck with two facts, seemingly contradictory, yet still indisputable. We see passing before us a wonderful display of courage, of activity, and of genius; an amazing prosperity is the result: we see a movement and a liberty unknown to the rest of Europe. But if we ask what was the real state of the inhabitants, how they passed their lives, what was their real share of happiness, the scene changes; there is perhaps no history so sad, so gloomy: no period, perhaps, during which the life of man appears to have been so agitated, subject to so many deplorable chances, and which so abounds in dissensions, crimes, and misfortunes. Another fact strikes us at the same moment: in the political life of the greater part of these republics, liberty was always growing less and less. The want of security was so great that the people were unavoidably driven to take shelter in a system less stormy, less popular, than that in which the State existed. Look at the history of Florence, Venice, Genoa, Milan, Pisa; in all of them we find the course of events, instead of aiding the progress of liberty, instead of enlarging the circle of institutions, tending to repress it; tending to concentrate power in the hands of a smaller number of individuals. In a word, we find in these republics, otherwise so energetic, so brilliant, and so rich, two things wanting—security of life, the first requisite in the social state, and the progress of institutions.

"From these causes spring a new evil, which prevented the attempt at republican organization from extending itself. It was from without—it was from foreign sovereigns—that the greatest danger was threatened to Italy. Still this danger never succeeded in reconciling the republics, in making them all act in concert; they were never ready to resist in common the common enemy. This has led many Italians, the most enlightened, the best patriots, to deplore, in the present day, the republican system of Italy in the middle ages, as the true cause which hindered it from becoming a nation; it was parceled out, they say, into a multitude of little States, not sufficiently master of their passions to confederate, to constitute themselves into one united body. The regret that the country has not, like the rest of Europe, been subjected to a despotic centralization which would have formed it into a nation, and rendered it independent of the foreigner.

"It appears, then, that republican organization, even

under the most favorable circumstances, did not contain, at this period, any more than it has done since, the principle of progress, duration, and extension. We may compare, up to a certain point, the organization of Italy, in the middle ages, to that of ancient Greece. Greece, like Italy, was a country covered with little republics, always rivals, sometimes enemies, and sometimes rallying together for a common object. In this comparison the advantage is altogether on the side of Greece. There is no doubt, notwithstanding the frequent iniquities that history makes known, but that there was much more order, security, and justice in the interior of Athens, Lacedæmon, and Thebes, than in the Italian republics. See, however, notwithstanding this, how short was the political career of Greece, and what a principle of weakness it contained in this parceling out of territory and power. No sooner did Greece come in contact with the great neighboring States, with Macedon and Rome, than she fell. These little republics, so glorious and still so flourishing, could not coalesce to resist. How much more likely was this to be the case in Italy, where society and human reason had made no such strides as in Greece, and consequently possessed much less power!"

This reads like what might have been the future history of the innumerable little republics which secession, if it were able, would set free on this continent. The ruin of the nations of antiquity was owing to the smallness of their extent. Their diminutive size exposed them almost exclusively to the influence of individual passions, and delivered them up a prey to those social vermin, the demagogues. One man could communicate his passions, from the stand of the orator, to the whole Athenian republic, and, in an instant, transport them into the wildest excesses.* The wars of the middle ages are attributable to pretty much the same cause. Greece, by the pure force of individual genius, rushed like a meteor to the zenith of power, blazed for a solitary instant in the dazzled eyes of the world, then sank in darkness forever: her society had no broad foundation in the full development of all the elements of human nature: the revolution of ideas was hindered by the overbearing influence of individual passions: in disturbing the empire of intelligence, they retarded its development. The same is true of all ancient communities. Troy, Carthage, and other nations, whose territorial extent was confined to little more than the mural limits of a city, were extinguished each by a single blow, and went out like falling stars. England was once a heptarchy, with seven kings and as many independent nations; and her life was a state of perpetual warfare, like that of kites and daws and wild beasts: nor was she an exaggerated type of most of the medieval States. Similar causes cannot produce dissimilar results: there is no reason to believe that this country, similarly partitioned, could escape a similar fate. Italy is only just now beginning to experience the commencement of that political convergence which alone can give her the importance which is her due among the great powers of the earth. At the same moment, and with such an example in her eyes, a portion of this already great and rising nation is spending her blood and treasure, with a prodigality which is without a precedent, in order to

* See M. Jouffroy on Philosophy of History.

reduce herself and the nation to the woeful plight from which Italy is escaping with so much difficulty.

But it is useless to run this parallel further, since it is morally and physically impossible that such a catastrophe can befall us in this age, when, by the laws of a political gravity, the most stupendous recombinations are taking place among the powers of the world, and when mighty empires alone can command that sense of security, permanence, and respect so dear to the heart of man. Happily, the nature of modern civilization and the laws of geography save us from the danger.

This process of decomposition was begun too soon or too late. It matters not now what may be the immediate verdict of this war: it may decide for or against the cause its martial arrays were impanneled to try: its ultimate consequences are quite another thing; *they* appear not in the fight; *they* summoned no armies to the field; no man thinks of them, or battles for them; but, while other issues occupy exclusive attention, while the poor motives of the immediate actors appear to direct the strife, they alone remain the last resolution, the imperishable residuum of the conflict. These ulterior consequences, so important but so invisible, depend not so much upon the will of man as upon the force of things; that force, which is sometimes called Providence, which leaves forever behind the past and determines the future, and by which the world is carried forward instead of backward, that force is beyond human control; all that man can do is to observe its movement and follow its direction: if he go counter to its tendency, he will be crushed by the collision; it still proceeds athwart human designs to its own ends.

The magnificent destiny of this nation is predetermined and inevitable. Its integrity is already placed beyond the reach of any man or set of men to destroy it. Though the nation be severed for a time, it will reunite in firmer bonds. It is borne to empire on the current of fate. The accumulated energies of many thousand years, of the entire past, are converging to its defense, and are pledged to its aggrandizement. Take courage, then, you whom Providence raises up in these wretched days. What seems to be the hour of dissolution, is but the beginning of a higher existence. A germ of future life is fermenting in the bosom of this corruption. The horrors we now witness are not the pangs of death, but the throes of a mighty parturition. Though it be amid the clash of arms, and millions be slain in obedience to the bloody rites of a barbarous ignorance, forth from this hecatomb of slaughtered victims will issue a new birth, which shall terminate the lawless interregnum of force, and renew the youth of humanity. This Avatar of the future, with which the womb of Time is now so rich, will come in the panoply of Peace; it will be the transformation of society; it will combine order with progress, conservatism with amelioration; it will give us LIBERTY WITH LAWS, AND GOVERNMENT WITHOUT OPPRESSION.

THE END.

www.ingramcontent.com/pod-product-compliance
Lightning Source LLC
LaVergne TN
LVHW010248110826
845151LV00004B/1415
9781425522742